BLOODY
HISTORY

MANCHESTER

BLOODY BRITISH HISTORY

HISTORY

MANCHESTER

MICHALA HULME

The
History
Press

For Mum and Dad,
who gave me the opportunity
to follow my dreams

First published in 2016

The History Press
The Mill, Brimscombe Port
Stroud, Gloucestershire, GL5 2QG
www.thehistorypress.co.uk

Reprinted in 2017

© Michala Hulme, 2016

The right of Michala Hulme to be identified as the Author
of this work has been asserted in accordance with the
Copyright, Designs and Patents Act 1988.

British Library Cataloguing in Publication Data.
A catalogue record for this book is available from the British Library.

ISBN 978 0 7509 6981 9

Typesetting and origination by The History Press
Printed in Great Britain

CONTENTS

ACKNOWLEDGEMENTS

I WOULD PERSONALLY like to thank Gavin Sterritt for his guidance and support whilst writing this book. I would also like to thank Alexanda Hulme and Rebecca Scott. A special mention must also go to Manchester Metropolitan University, GMP Police Museum and Manchester City Council for their help on this project.

ABOUT THE AUTHOR

MICHALA HULME IS a historian and genealogist from Cheshire. She studied the history of Manchester at MMU as part of a BA (Hons) degree. Her thesis, entitled 'The Origins and Early Years of Philip's Park Cemetery', was shortlisted for Best Dissertation in Regional and Local History. She is currently in the process of completing a PhD.

As well as being the owner of Unearth the Past, a history research company, she has written for *Who Do You Think You Are?* magazine and can be heard regularly on BBC local radio.

She is the author of *A Grim Almanac of Manchester* for The History Press.

For more information about Michala please check out her website:

www.michalahulme.com

AD 77–410

'MAMUCIUM'

BEFORE THE ROMANS arrived on British shores, the city of Manchester would have been unrecognisable to the modern Mancunian eye. To begin with it wasn't called 'Manchester'. The terrain was marshy and uneven, with streams running down the familiar places we know today as Market Street, Deansgate and through the Market Place. The land was immersed by a dense forest, which would prove the perfect shelter when the Romans finally attacked in AD 79.

According to Roman historians, Mancunium or Mamucium as they called it, was under the direction of the Celtic Brigantes tribe, who controlled most of the northern territories. The Celts were a warlike people, and would frequently fight with other tribes. They were ruled by

The Romans building a fort at Mancenion in AD 80, by Ford Madox Brown. (With the kind permission of Manchester City Council)

a king, queen or chief. When they weren't fighting, the Celts would farm the land and tend to their crops. Two sub-division tribes called the Voluntii and the Sistuntii occupied the area to the west of Britain, which included parts of Lancashire and the Lake District. It is therefore probable that 'Manchester' fell into their territory. It is likely that the tribe settled in Manchester because it was naturally well defended, with three deep streams and a large bank that would protect the natives from attacks by other tribes.

When Julius Caesar arrived in Britain in 55 BC, the northern territories were probably unaware of his presence – the great British weather stopped him getting any further than Brentford. It would be another 100 years before the Romans reached the North West.

Under the reign of the Emperor Claudius, the Romans managed to put parts of Britain under the control of Rome. This was done by force and by wooing the tribal chiefs, taking them or their sons to Rome to show them the life they could have if they co-operated. Some tribes decided to show their alliance to the Romans, whereas others, such as Queen Boudicca, decided that she and her army would not go down without a fight. After a bloody uprising, and fearing defeat, she took her own life.

On 13 June AD 40, a Roman senator named Lucius Julius Graecinus and his wife Julia Procilla welcomed a son named Gnaeus Julius Agricola. Agricola was born into a prominent Roman family – both his grandfathers were Imperial governors. Not long after his birth, his father was murdered by the Roman Emperor, leaving him to be brought up by his mother. As a child, his mother sent him to school in Marseille, France, where he developed a love of philosophy. Agricola's military career began as a tribune under the direction of Paulinus in Britain. Paulinus and his men arrived in the country in AD 58 and stayed until AD 62. Agricola's time in Britain, getting to know the tribes, would pay dividends later on in his career. In AD 69, the Romans were in the midst of a civil war. Agricola took the side of Vespasian. It is believed that he aligned himself with the future Emperor after his mother was murdered on the family estate by Otho's men. Vespasian rewarded Agricola by removing Marcus Roscius Coelius

A statue of Manchester's Roman founder Gnaeus Julius Agricola is proudly displayed above the main archway of the Town Hall.

A Roman camp similar to the original camp set up in Manchester.

from the post of commander of an army in Britain and replacing him with the loyal Agricola. Agricola's job in Britain was to take authority of any settlements that were still controlled by tribal leaders.

In AD 78, Agricola and his men arrived on British soil. By AD 79, he and his army had reached Deva (Chester). After establishing a fort in the town, Agricola advanced west, passing near Northwich into Streford before finally reaching the River Medlock near Knott Mill. When he arrived it is believed that he attacked the native Britons and forced them into exile in the surrounding woods. Agricola decided that Mamucium would be the ideal place to station his army, being strategically well situated between the military bases in Chester and York. The first fort was built on a 5-acre site near where the River Irwell met the Medlock, now known as Castlefield. It was constructed using timber with reinforced turf banks lined with stakes. Between AD 90–200 the fort was modified and strengthened.

The north gate was rebuilt, and most of the wood structures were replaced with stone. A road was built from the northeast into the fort. It was made out of small stones with two ditches either side of it. The Romans also constructed the A56 Chester Road, as it is known today. It stretched from Mamucium towards Deva (Chester).

As the years progressed, a substantial vicus – Roman neighbourhood – grew outside of the walls of the fort. The vicus housed the families of the Roman army and contained shops, storehouses and furnaces, thus providing facilities for making weapons for the garrison. Archaeological finds suggest that the vicus stretched towards the area now known as Old Trafford and towards Deansgate. It is also possible that it reached Hulme. The civilian population would have lived in single-storey timber buildings made with a clay floor that would have been covered in straw. Evidence suggests that between 600 and 1,000 troops could have lived in the fort.

Mamucium remained under the sovereignty of the Romans for the next 300 years. It formed part of the province of Maxima Caesariensis. When their departure eventually occurred, it was not altogether celebrated by the Anglo-Roman residents, who had prospered and been protected by the ruling force – the Romans had successfully defended the town and its inhabitants from a vicious attack by the Picts and the Scots. The residents were also immersed in the Roman way of life, using the currency and practicing their religion.

The Romans left at the beginning of the fifth century, when they were called back to Italy to protect the country from the Barbarian invasion. Those that stayed behind merged with the local farming community. The only visible part of the fort that remains today is a small section of the south-east gateway which can be found under arch 95 of the viaduct. The rest of the fort was destroyed over the years, due to the complete redevelopment of Castlefield. A statue of Agricola – 'Manchester's founding father' – can be found over the main archway of the Town Hall.

In 1982 a group of archaeologists recreated the original camp in Manchester. This is what the north gate would have looked like in AD 200.

AD 430–800

THE LEGEND OF TARQUIN AND THE BLOODY SAXONS

THE ROMANS LEFT Mamucium in the first half of the fifth century. The fort, which was constructed where the River Irwell met the Medlock, was adapted into a castle, with curved stone walls and two watchtowers which were erected either side of the gated entrance. The castle became known by the residents of the town as 'Tarquin's Castle'. Legend has it that after the departure of the Romans, castles were being built across the country and they were inhabited by British knights. Fearing invasion from the Picts and Scots, the knights invited the Saxons to help them destroy the enemy. The Saxons travelled from northern Germany, Demark and the Netherlands across the North Sea, arriving on the shores of Britain in wooden boats. They first tried to land here during the Roman occupation, however they were beaten back by the occupying forces.

The assistance provided by the Saxons after the Romans had left didn't quite go to plan. The Saxons, who had other ideas, seized the natives' land for themselves and evicted the knights from their castles. Manchester's castle was surrendered in AD 488.

One man who was unhappy about the behaviour of the Saxons was King Arthur. Arthur gathered his knights and fought tirelessly to stop the Saxons advancing. The king met with his knights around a round table in Camelot. The story has it that the leader of the Knights of the Round Table was a man named Sir Lancelot Du Lac. In one of Lancelot's quests he rescued a fellow knight named Gawaine (or Gawin) from an evil knight named Sir Carados. In the midst of the battle Lancelot killed Carados. Sometime later, Sir Tarquin – brother to Carados and enemy of Arthur – kidnapped some of Lancelot's fellow Knights of the Round Table including his nephew, Sir Lionel. According to the Manchester legend, the prisoners were held at Tarquin's castle, which was in Manchester. Tarquin was the worst of all the evil knights. He was described as a giant whose appetite for cruelty was only matched by his towering stature. When Lancelot reached Tarquin's castle, he hit a basin, which was hanging on a tree outside, and summoned the wicked knight and his company to a fight. Tarquin had foreseen that Lancelot

was going to attempt to rescue the prisoners and was waiting for his arrival.
Tarquin, followed by his men, met
Lancelot outside of his castle and the
pair duelled. The fight allegedly lasted
for hours. Lancelot was eventually
declared the winner after he managed
to chop Tarquin's head off, seize the
castle and rescue the imprisoned
knights. Over time, the story has expe-
rienced many reincarnations. Although
there is no actual proof that Tarquin or
Lancelot existed, the outline of the story
may have some truth in Manchester.
Historians have claimed that the story
of Tarquin, the cruel giant in the castle,
is a depiction of the Angles who took
over the occupation of the town after
the Romans departed. The Angles were
not seen as 'fair' leaders; they allegedly dished out cruel treatment on the
town's Romano-British residents.

*A depiction of the famous knight
Sir Lancelot Du Lac.*

The legend of King Arthur, Lancelot
and the Knights of the Round Table,
with their heroic quests to stop the
Saxon invasion, gripped the imagina-
tion of the British public. During the
nineteenth century there was a revival
of the tales, with the release of an array
of new books and art on the subject.
In 1880, Chetham's Hospital had on
display a picture of Tarquin, about to
eat a 'plump' Manchester child.

Legends aside, the Saxons would
dominate the British landscape for the
next 600 years. The town's history
under the Saxons is somewhat sketchy
and contradicting. The *Historical Reader*
suggests that a Saxon chief called

Ebissa governed the town, although
little else is known about his reign.
There is a thought that he came over
to Britain with Octa, the later Anglo-
Saxon King of Kent. During the sixth
century, Manchester formed part of
Northumberland under the reign of King
Aethelfrith. After his death, the throne
was passed to Edwin, who was the son
of King Alle of Deira. It is believed that
he introduced 'Manigeceaster' – as it
was now known – to Christianity. After
his own baptism in 627, many villagers
and townsfolk converted from their own
religion to Christianity. To accommo-
date the 'new' religion, Manchester built
St Michael's church in Aldport. A few
years later a church called St Mary's
was built at Acres Field.

1596–1608

THE DOCTOR AND THE DEVIL

ON 18 FEBRUARY 1516, at Greenwich Palace, London, King Henry VIII and his wife Catherine of Aragon welcomed their first child, a beautiful red-haired daughter named Mary. Her arrival was probably somewhat of a disappointment to her father, who had his heart set on a boy who would become his heir. After seventeen years of trying, no heir followed Mary. The king took the decision to annul his marriage to Catherine and wed Ann Boleyn, who was Catherine's lady-in-waiting. In annulling his marriage, he automatically declared his daughter Mary illegitimate.

Following the death of Henry VIII in 1547, Mary's half-brother Edward VI – born in 1537 – had a brief stint on the throne. Edward, though, died six years after his coronation, leaving the throne vacant. Lady Jane Grey was the preferred choice by some, however Mary was not going to be overlooked. She marched her army to London where she gained support from the nobility and ruling classes and cemented her place as the new queen. She was crowned on 1 October 1553. After her coronation, Mary placed her half-sister Elizabeth in the Tower of London.

Queen Mary, like her father and grandfather before her, hired an astrologer to serve in her court. The queen chose one of the country's greatest thinkers, who was also an eminent doctor, astrologer and mathematician named John Dee.

Dee was born on 13 July 1527. The astrologer was no stranger to royal courts – his father Rowland was a gentleman's usher in the court of King Henry VIII. In 1544, Dee attained a degree from St John's College, Cambridge, and two years later he was awarded a fellowship from Trinity College. After graduating, Dee travelled across Europe lecturing, before eventually returning to London.

Portrait of John Dee.

In 1553, Dee was called to speak to Elizabeth in the Tower of London. Elizabeth wanted the astrologer to tell her when her sister Mary was going to die. When the queen learned of his actions she was furious and accused him of trying to murder her through sorcery. He was at once placed in jail. The queen eventually pardoned him, however he was thrown in jail again in 1555 for heresy.

In 1558, Mary died and Elizabeth replaced her as queen. Dee was appointed as her personal astrologer and she consulted him on a whole array of matters. His love of experiments earned him the title of the 'Court Conjuror'.

Twenty years after his appointment, Dee met a fellow astrologer named Edward Kelley. The pair became friends, and with their families in tow they went travelling across Europe. Kelley fancied himself as a bit of a medium, and Kelley and Dee began to dabble in the supernatural. It was alleged that the pair used crystal balls to talk to angels. Dee, however, was not comfortable with Kelley's practices and doubted the authenticity of his work. He decided that he was going to return home but, once back, found that his house and laboratory had been burned down by an angry mob who disagreed with his practices. With no money and a sketchy reputation for using occult practices, Dee reached out to his trusted ally Elizabeth for help. In 1595, she managed to secure him the position of Warden of the Manchester Colligate Church, replacing Dr Chadderton who had taken up the role of Bishop of Chester. Dee accepted the offer – although he would have much preferred a position in the South. The astrologer and his family moved to the town in February 1596.

Dee performing one of his experiments in front of Queen Elizabeth I.

Dee took up residency in Christ's College (now Chetham's School) and engaged himself in Church life. He also began working as a surgeon. The rumours and accusations that caused him to flee from his former home, however, followed him to Manchester. Within a year of moving to the town, Dee was summoned to help the 'Lancashire Seven'. In 1595, two children named John and Ann Starkie began to convulse. Their parents were so concerned for their health that they spent £200 trying to find a cure. When all hope was fading, they sought the services of a Catholic priest, who thought that they might be possessed. The parents decided to consult a local 'wiseman' named Edmund Hartley, who, for a fee, managed to keep the children's condition at bay by using alternative therapies. A year after Hartley's arrival other members of the household began to get struck down by this mystery illness. The sick patients began to howl, shout, scream, shake and hold their breath till they turned blue. The parents of the ill children claimed that Hartley had made them mad by possessing them with the Devil by kissing them. He was subsequently brought up at the Lancashire Assize and was found guilty of witchcraft. He was sentenced to death by hanging. However, his execution didn't quite go to plan. The rope snapped and Edward – still alive – fell to the floor. Not wanting to be beaten a second time, the hangman made sure that the rope was fully secure and he was hung again, this time successfully.

The Starkies now decided to approach the great mind of John Dee. Famed for his occult practices, if anyone could cure them, Dee could. However, Dee refused. Instead he put the family in touch with a Puritan minister and exorcist named John Darrell. Darrell worked his magic and all but one of the afflicted appeared to be cured. In Manchester, Dee could not escape his reputation for witchcraft and trying to contact demons – it didn't help that he had written books on the subject. Throughout his time in the town, he was constantly at battle with the congregation of the church and faced persecution from members of the college, who did not like his choice of sermons and some of his personal beliefs. They claimed that a scorch mark on the table in one of the audit rooms at the college was a hoof print from Satan, summoned by Dee. In an attempt to clear his name, he wrote to the new king, James I, however his petition fell on deaf ears and he was forced to move back to Surrey in disgrace. As Dee and his family were getting ready to leave Manchester, a deadly plague struck the town, claiming the lives of his wife and two daughters. Dee returned to Surrey a broken man. He died in poverty in 1608.

1581–1645

THE PLAGUES

DURING THE LATTER half of the sixteenth century Manchester was ravaged by a series of deadly plagues. Although the specific strain of these plagues are unknown, it is believed that they were a form of the bubonic plague. Several epidemics thrived during this period. Poor sanitation, coupled with poor harvests, had left people weak and susceptible to illness. The free movement of people between villages and towns to find employment helped the bacterial epidemic to spread. The plague originated in Asia. It is thought that infected fleas, carried on rats, came over to Central Europe and then Britain, via trade ships. The bacteria was then passed on to humans who came into contact with the infected rats. Symptoms usually consisted of chills, vomiting of blood, high fever, coughing, gangrene, muscle cramps and the painful large swelling of the lymph glands, which often burst causing pus to seep out of the open wound.

The first recorded plague in Manchester during this period was in 1581. This was followed by a plague described as a 'dreadful epidemic' in 1587. In 1590, the plague took hold again, this time killing seventy people in one month. However, the worst plague occurred in 1605, claiming the lives of over 1,000 people. It is thought that the epidemic had spread from Chester, which had suffered terribly from the plague during the years 1603–05. Manchester's plague was at its worst during the months of April to October. In March 1605, the number of deaths in Manchester was ten, by August this had increased to over 230. The death rate for that year stood at 1,078. In 1604 the figure was only 188. Amongst the dead was the college chaplain, Mr Kirk, his wife and four children.

By May 1605, Justices of the Peace and the town constables of Manchester applied a tax to those people who they believed could afford it. Anyone who refused to pay the tax would be put in jail until it was paid. The money from the tax would go towards a relief fund for those that were showing symptoms and those that were diagnosed with the plague.

Two victims of the plague.

Anyone found to be suffering from the plague and still at home was entitled to 1s per week. If a person was suffering and had been moved to Collyhurst Common, a hospital for plague victims, they would be afforded 1s 4d per week. During the month of August 1605, 210 people were receiving relief at home.

Sir Rowland Mosley, who had taken over from his father as the new lord of the manor in the first half of the sixteenth century, had provided the 6-acre piece of land on Collyhurst Common. The land was fitted with huts that would keep plague victims quarantined from the rest of the inhabitants. Mosley also provided a burial ground, which basically consisted of a big hole where the plague victims would be wrapped in a grave cloth and then covered with earth.

Anyone found to be infected with the disease was put under strict sanctions, which it was hoped would stop the epidemic from spreading. One of the restrictions was that the infected person had to keep their house in order. If they refused, the watchman had permission to use violence to force them to oblige. Another restriction placed on the infected was that they were not permitted to socialise, and any person caught doing so would be charged as a felon and faced the death penalty. One such rebel was Philip Fitton of Moston. Fitton, who was infected with the disease, showed no respect for the sanctions placed upon him. He openly went to infected houses and wore the cast-off clothing of plague victims. After giving the constables the runaround, he was eventually apprehended and sent to the dungeon.

The outfit commonly worn by doctors treating the plague.

The town's officials also stopped all christenings and weddings throughout the months that the plague was at its height. It was hoped that if public gatherings were cancelled, the plague would not spread. Along with those that lived in Manchester, there were also restrictions on anyone coming into the town. Five people who resided in Nantwich – which had also suffered with the plague during this period – had to produce a document signed by the mayor and twenty-five other people in the town to say that they were clear of the disease.

After this episode, the plague seems to have given the town some respite, as it was another forty years before the epidemic was recorded again. The plague that occurred in the summer of 1645 caused the authorities to take action. Estimates suggest that this plague caused the mortality rate to increase six-fold and left no part of the town 'unvisited'. In total just over a quarter of the population died because of the plague. In an attempt to control the disease, the town's officials again stopped all people leaving and entering the town and the market was also cancelled.

The victims of the plague were buried in a large pit which was then covered with earth.

1595–1641

THE SCREAMING SKULL OF WARDLEY HALL

EDWARD BARLOW WAS born in Chorlton-cum-Hardy in 1595. He was the fourth son of wealthy landowner Sir Alexander Barlow and his wife Mary Brereton, whose family owned Handforth Hall. The Barlows lived in the opulent Barlow Hall. On 30 November 1595, Edward was christened at the local parish church in Didsbury. The Barlow family were practising Catholics, however due to the Reformation they were forced to convert.

Throughout the sixteenth century, England's relationship with religion shifted between the Pope and the Church of England. At the beginning of the century, Henry VIII took the decision to part ways with Rome after Pope Clement VII refused to annul his marriage to Catherine of Aragon. However, it would be under the guidance of his son, King Edward VI, who was brought up a Protestant, that the authorities would really clamp down on anyone or anything that represented Catholicism. In towns and villages across the country, stained-glass windows were destroyed, and statues and memorials were defaced. When Mary – a Catholic – took to the throne in 1553, she attempted to build bridges with the Pope by repealing the Reformation legislation. She reintroduced Catholic doctrines, and replaced the statues, lecterns and stained-glass windows. During a four-year period she executed over 300 Protestants, earning her the title 'Bloody Mary'. This brief return to Catholicism was short lived, however. In 1558, Mary died childless. With no heirs, the next in line for the throne was her half-sister Elizabeth, the only daughter of Ann Boleyn. Elizabeth was not born a Catholic and could not follow Catholicism – if she did it would make her illegitimate. The new queen banned all masses; anyone caught attending would face a hefty fine or imprisonment. During her reign, any Catholic priests caught delivering mass faced the prospect of execution. Throughout the country, Catholic landed gentry built priest holes in their houses to hide the religious rebel preachers.

Edward's grandfather was one of those who refused to conform. He died while imprisoned for his religious beliefs. Edward's father, Alexander, had a large proportion of his land seized because he too was reluctant to join the

Protestant faith. Edward, however, was born a Protestant. When he was in his teens, he left England and travelled to Europe to pursue his studies. He began his schooling in Douai, France, before moving to Spain. By this time Edward had received his 'calling', and decided that he wanted to study Catholicism and become a priest. After returning to Douai in 1616, he joined the Order of Saint Benedict and was ordained the following year.

Statue of Ambrose Barlow.
(Sjukmidlands, Wikimedia Commons)

Upon returning to England, Ambrose Barlow – as he was now known – began to preach in Manchester. Barlow had several skirmishes with the law and was imprisoned at least four times for his preachings. During the 1630s, Barlow was conducting illegal masses in the areas that are known today as Leigh and Worsley. While in Leigh it is believed that he stayed at Morley Hall, the home of Sir Thomas Tyldesley who was a recusant. Tyldesley allowed Barlow to hold masses at Morley Hall for the Leigh parishioners.

At the beginning of 1641, King Charles I issued a warning to all priests stating that they must leave the country or face being treated as a traitor with the prospect of being executed. On Easter Sunday, 25 April, of the same year, Barlow was conducting one of his religious services when a mob armed with sticks, led by the Vicar of Leigh, marched to the house and seized the priest. He was transferred to Lancaster Castle. On 7 September 1641 he was brought up in front of Sir Robert Heath and was found guilty of being a traitor to the king. Heath sentenced Barlow to death, an act designed to deter other Catholic priests. Three days later Barlow was stripped, hung and quartered. His head was then removed and placed on a spike outside the Collegiate Church in Manchester.

The owner of Wardley Hall, a man named Roger Downes, managed to get possession of the skull – it is believed that Barlow had previously conducted a mass at the house. Downes placed the skull in a glass case and hid it in a recess at the top of the stairs. Downes then wrote in the lease that whoever

Wardley Hall, otherwise known as 'Skull House', still houses the skull of St Ambrose Barlow.

took over the ownership of the house must keep the skull in its original case. For the following 200 years, the skull stayed in its place – it is alleged that it was forgotten about. One day, during the nineteenth century, a maid, who was working in the house, found the skull and decided that she was going to throw it in the moat. That night the most almighty storm battered the house. Fearing supernatural powers from the skull were causing it, the maid confessed to what she had done. The owners of the house demanded that the moat be emptied and the skull be placed back in its original case. Over the years the house was sold to different owners and the skull was moved. However, it was not long before it was back in its case, as, every time it was moved, the tale goes that chaos and unrest swept through the house. The skull became known as

the 'screaming skull' and Wardley Hall earned itself the nickname 'Skull House'.

In 1960, a scientific examination was held on the skull to see if it really was that of Ambrose Barlow. The scientist involved confirmed that the skull was of a man 50–60 years old, which puts it in the same age bracket as Barlow. Using pictures, it was also evident that the skull had the same bone structure at the priest. The scientist also found evidence that some kind of sharp instrument had been driven through the head, which matched that of a spike. Therefore, it was officially acknowledged by the Catholic community including the bishop, that the skull was that of Ambrose Barlow. In 1970, Ambrose, along with forty priests who were martyred during the Reformation, were canonised by Pope Paul VI. He is now known as Saint Ambrose Barlow.

1642

THE MANCHESTER SIEGE

DURING THE ENGLISH civil wars Manchester was attacked three times. The wars (1642–1651) – principally a disagreement between the king, Charles I, and his Long Parliament – split the country into those that supported the king (Cavaliers) and those that supported Parliament (Roundheads). Manchester – along with most other northern towns – took the side of the Roundheads.

On 4 July 1642, Manchester received word that the Cavaliers, led by Lord Strange, were en-route to the town to seize their magazine (gunpowder). Strange, the son of William, Earl of Derby, had been appointed by the king as the Lord Lieutenant of the counties of Lancaster and Chester. He, along with a number of armed men, had managed to seize a magazine from Liverpool and were now on their way to deal the same fate to Manchester.

As Strange and his group of Cavaliers approached Manchester, they sent a messenger to the town requesting ten barrels of gunpowder. If the residents refused, the Lord Lieutenant would 'make them yield and bring them to subjection'. However, the inhabitants refused, stating that it was the only defence they had and they would risk their lives to save it. Furious with their response, Strange gathered his men and marched into the town. Upon arriving at Deansgate, the men fired their muskets and demanded the magazine, however it was all in vain because the quick-thinking townspeople had removed the gunpowder from the store and had hidden it in the college. Unable to get his hands on the magazine, Strange and his men left for Bury.

As the news spread of Strange's dealings with Manchester and fearing another attack was imminent, Parliament sent reinforcements to Manchester. Sir Thomas Stanley, Richard Holland, Mr Holcroft, Mr Egerton, Mr Booth, Mr Ashton and Mr Moore headed north to help to oppose Lord Strange.

On 15 July 1642, Strange was invited to a banquet in the town. He brought with him a large army of 400 men.

In the nineteenth century, Ford Madox Brown (1821–1893) painted 'Bradshaw's Defence of Manchester, AD 1642', which shows the victory of the town's forces against the Royalists.
(With the kind permission of Manchester City Council)

Whilst he was dining, Captain Birch and Captain Holcroft rode into Manchester with their army and were greeted by the Royalist militia. A battle then erupted between the two parties. In the midst of the fighting, a linen weaver from Kirkmanshulme named Richard Percival was killed by the Royalist forces. It is widely believed that this was the first death of the Civil War. After the skirmish had finished, Strange and his men retreated into Cheshire.

On 14 September 1642, Sir Robert Harley read an impeachment of high treason in the House of Commons against Lord Strange for his dealings in Manchester. However, the Parliamentarians knew that Lord Strange would not willingly come to answer the charge, so they sent out a warning that anyone found to be helping Strange with men, funding, food and ammunition would themselves be guilty of treason.

While Parliament was impeaching Strange, the residents of Manchester were preparing themselves for another attack. The ruling Parliamentarians of the town employed the services of a German captain named John Roseworme for a cost of £30. Roseworme ensured that the townspeople had training with the militia, which assisted them to become 'active pikesmen'. The town was fortified with mud walls, chains and fortification posts at the end of all of the streets. The townsmen also enlisted the help of local country people, who were prepared to fight with the Roundheads. With the town prepared for war, all they could do was wait.

On the night of Saturday, 24 September 1642, word reached Manchester that Lord Strange and Lord Molineaux were

Portrait of Lord Strange, 7th Earl of Derby.
(Wikimedia Commons)

marching from Warrington to the town. Strange would be bringing with him an army of 4,000 foot soldiers, 200 dragoons, 100 light horses and seven cannons.

The town's forces, led by Captain Radcliffe, got into position on the south side of the town. Radcliffe then turned to his men and delivered a rousing speech, stating they would maintain their freedom and property at all costs. Not long after Radcliffe had finished talking, the bells of the church rang, which gave warning that the Cavaliers had entered the town. As the Cavaliers marched up Deansgate and spilt into two groups, one fraction stationed themselves on the south side of the city, at the house of Edward Mosley, and the other group marched along the opposite bank of the Mersey and Irwell towards Salford.

The men retained their positions throughout the night and on the following morning two men from

Manchester approached Strange to enquire why he had arrived in the town with such force. Not taking kindly to the two messengers, Strange decided to take one of them hostage and sent the other back with a message to the town's forces stating that he was coming to take the town in the name of the king.

The forces continued their stand-off till Monday lunchtime, when, under a blanket of heavy rain, the Cavaliers began to unleash their firepower on Deansgate. Chaos then commenced as the two sides went into battle. Manchester suffered greatly during the fight. Homes and barns were ransacked, looted and set on fire.

However, after several days of fighting, the town's militia, led by Captain Bradshaw, made great gains, forcing Strange and his Royalist men to retreat into Salford. Strange and his army had suffered heavy casualties with the loss of 200 men – three of these are said to be buried in Didsbury. By the Saturday, a request was made to exchange prisoners. After this was complete, a cease-fire was declared and Lord Strange left the area and went to stay at a house in Latham. Manchester's defiance and bravery against the Royalists was seen as a great victory and morale boost for the Roundheads' campaign. The town, which had suffered three attacks during the Civil War, became the headquarters for the Roundheads and remained loyal to Parliament.

Lord Strange, who later became the 7th Earl of Derby, was captured near Nantwich and was tried in Chester, where he was found guilty of treason. Strange was sentenced to death by hanging. He was transferred to Bolton and hung in the Churchgate on 15 October 1651. He was buried in Ormskirk church.

1661

THE TRAITOROUS GHOST AND THE HORSESHOE

ON 23 APRIL 1661, the people of Manchester were celebrating the coronation of Charles II, which had taken place earlier that day at Westminster Abbey. Charles had been declared king by the English Parliament in 1660, following the death of Oliver

A depiction of the mysterious spirit who warned that the king was going to be murdered.

Cromwell some two years previously. Charles was hiding in the Netherlands when Cromwell died. He had left England by boat whilst disguised as a manservant following his defeat at the Battle of Worcester in 1651 to the Roundheads, and to avoid capture he hid under an oak tree. However, in 1660 Parliament sent a ship to pick up the king and his court – which included his beloved spaniels.

The restoration of Charles II as monarch was received with joy and elation in Manchester. A military procession was led by Major John Byrom, Nicholas Mosley and their troops in support of the new king. The men marched to the Collegiate Church where a Royalist service was delivered by the churchwarden. Fireworks and bonfires could be seen across the town. A public dinner was held for the residents and it was said that for one night only the water supply delivered wine and not water. While the majority of townsfolk were joining in the celebrations, however, there were some who did not support the new king.

Only a few years after his coronation, Charles II introduced the highly unpopular Hearth Tax. Money from the tax was used to pay the king's debt. The 2s tax was levied on every home with two or more hearths or stoves. The money was payable by the tenant and not the landlord. In Manchester it was reported that 1,368 people were eligible for the tax. Edward Byrom, who lived in the Shambles, paid 12s in taxes.

Even after the introduction of the tax, history would argue that Charles II was one of the more 'popular' kings during this period. However, this did not stop the king and his court being surrounded by an atmosphere of unrest and disloyalty. Treason carried the most severe punishment in the land – death – and rewards were offered to those that 'outed' potential traitors.

Not long after the king was crowned, a Stockport shoemaker was brought to Manchester on a charge of treason. It was alleged that the man had made a sweeping statement to the effect that the king would only reign for three years before he converted to a Papist – a Catholic follower of the Pope – and would be murdered by someone in his house. When the man was brought up in front of Nicholas Mosley, the magistrate, he denied all the charges. The shoemaker claimed that he had heard the story from a local woman. He stated that the woman was cleaning the floor of an inn when she accidently knocked a knife on the floor. Despite searching high and low she couldn't find it. Eventually she decided to look under the floorboards. After lifting up one of the boards she came across the bones of a man. She then said that a green spirit visited her in the room. She told the shoemaker that the spirit told her that a murder had occurred in the house some thirteen years previous and one of the culprits – a woman – was still at large. In order to put the spirit to rest, the shoemaker must seek justice for the murdered victim. While there, she also stated that the shoemaker had a message that must be delivered: the king and two of his servants would convert to Catholicism and follow the guidance of the Pope, but his two servants – who the king thought were loyal – would then kill him. Such was the remarkable nature of the story that the magistrate referred it to the quarter sessions.

Also heard at the sessions, Mosley blamed drink on the reason one man had stated that the Devil could take the king, and prosecuted another man from Pendleton who it was claimed was a 'wiseman and fortune teller'. The 'wiseman', named John Rushton, had been called upon by a woman who thought that her child may have been 'hurt by an evil tongue'. Rushton confirmed that this may be the case and gave the woman two horseshoes and three nails. He told her to fasten one of the horseshoes to her door with the nails, as it would ward off evil spirits and save the child from death. After several weeks nothing happened, and the child remained sick. Rushton, who was outed as a fraud, was sent to the sessions.

1745

THE RISING OF '45

ON 31 DECEMBER 1720, James Francis Edward Stuart and Clementina Sobieska welcomed their first son Charles Edward Stuart into the world. At the time of Charles's birth, his parents were living as guests of the Pope. James Stuart despised the British monarchy. He had served in the French army against the British and after the death of Queen Anne he participated in a series of planned uprisings to raise the Jacobite flag in Scotland and England.

Portrait of Bonnie Prince Charlie.
(Wikimedia Commons)

After all these attempts failed, he headed to Rome where he was reluctantly welcomed as a guest of the Pope. He remained in Rome up until his death in 1766.

James's son was brought up with the same values as his father, however he had ambition and age on his side. In July 1745, Charles, who would later be known as Bonnie Prince Charlie or the Young Pretender, decided he was going to attempt to overthrow the British monarchy. At the age of 24, and with only seven men, he left France and landed in the Hebrides, in the hope of raising an army. The Young Pretender succeeded in gathering support from his Scottish allies and the Stuart standard was raised at Glenfinnan.

While Bonnie Prince Charlie and his army were growing in size and confidence, word filtered down to Manchester that the Jacobite army had entered England and were going to travel through the North West on their way to London.

On 26 November, Charlie and his army had reached Preston. Having heard that he was coming and with reports that he was travelling with a party of between 10,000 and 30,000 men, the people of Preston had taken measures to try and protect their families and businesses, with many families fleeing the area, shops closed and warehouses emptied.

Manchester had more sympathy for the Jacobite cause than Preston and didn't go to such extreme lengths to protect the town.

On 28 November, a Scottish sergeant and a drummer from Halifax arrived in Manchester. The Highlanders had come to inform the residents that Bonnie Prince Charlie would be arriving the following day. The men were also there to recruit volunteers to join the Jacobite army. All interested men were offered a 5 guinea advance, with 1s paid on the day and the rest to be paid when Bonnie Prince Charlie arrived. At the end of the day, the messengers had managed to recruit 180 officers. Included in that number was a linen draper named John Beswick. Beswick was born in Manchester in 1721. His family were reasonably wealthy and were supporters of the Jacobites – his uncle died in exile while supporting the Stuarts. Also to sign up that day were the three sons of eminent surgeon Dr Deacon. Deacon and his sons Robert, Charles and Thomas were also Jabcobite sympathisers. Another recruit was a barber named Thomas Sydall. Sydall's father had taken part in the rebellion of 1715, which led to his execution the

Prince Charlie's vanguard at Manchester.

following year in Manchester. All the new recruits would take their position in the Manchester Regiment under the direction of Colonel Francis Towneley.

From 10 a.m. the following morning, the Young Pretender's troops began to arrive in Manchester in their Highland dress armed with swords and rifles. Charlie did not ride into the town until 2 p.m., when he took up residence at the home of John Dickinson on Market Street. He remained there until the following day, when he left to attend a service preached by Thomas Cappock at the Collegiate Church. After the service, he inspected the 300 men of the Manchester Regiment in front of a large crowd. The Young Pretender remained in Manchester until 1 December 1745, when he left to carry on his journey to London.

Charles got as far as Derby before retreating back North. On 9 December, a message was sent to Manchester stating that he and his troops were on their way back. At 2 p.m. the first of the troops arrived back in the town. Unlike the previous visit, where the troops had been welcomed, the attitudes of the people had now changed. An angry mob, which was waiting for the Jacobite army, began attacking them with mud and stones. The mob was warned that if they did not surrender they would be shot and killed. Fearing for their lives, the mob retreated. The troops then issued a warning to the residents of the town to state that any persons found walking in groups of more than two would be deemed as rioters and would be punished.

The following day, an order was received from the Young Pretender demanding a contribution of £5,000 for the distress caused by the mob.

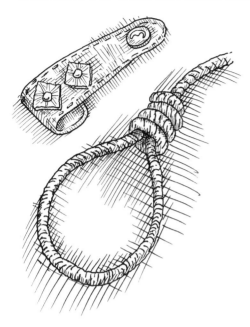

None of the Manchester officers could
escape the hangman's rope: they were
executed at Kennington Common.

The people of Manchester had till one 1 p.m. to raise the money. To ensure payment, the troops seized a wealthy merchant named James Bayley, who lived in a large house on the corner of St Anne's Square. After a series of negotiations, Bayley managed to secure his release on condition that he raised £2,500 by 1 p.m. Bayley went to a local coffee shop, where he and another man named John Dickinson secured the money by offering promise notes that the donors' money would be paid back within three months. The money was then given to the prince at 2 p.m. In the meantime word had reached the Pretender that the Duke of Cumberland and his army were marching south. Without haste, the prince and his troops – which included the Manchester Regiment – continued on their journey north.

The troops marched through Lancaster and arrived at Carlisle on 19 December, where they started fighting with the Duke of Cumberland's troops. With severe losses to Charlie's army, he eventually decided to retreat back to Scotland, deserting the remaining 143 men of the Manchester Regiment, who were handed over to the Duke of Cumberland. All of the captured officers were transferred to London, while the rest of the ranks were split between gaols in Penrith, Kendal and Carlisle.

The townsfolk of Manchester celebrated the victory of Cumberland's army by illuminating windows. Effigies of the Young Pretender were paraded across the town. An angry mob of Presbyterians marched up and down the streets, breaking windows that were not lit. Dr Deacon, who refused to light his windows, was set upon by the mob, who threatened him and told him to leave the town before smashing all of his windows.

The trial of the officers began in July 1746 and lasted for three days; all were found guilty of treason. On 30 July, Colonel Francis Towneley, Captain Deacon, Captain James Dawson, Lieutenant John Beswick, Captain George Fletcher, Captain

The heads of Deacon, Chadwick and Sydall
were brought back to Manchester and
placed on stakes outside the Exchange.

James Blood, Captain David Morgan, Lieutenant Thomas Chadwick and Adjutant Thomas Sydall were executed on Kennington Common. The heads of Deacon, Chadwick and Sydall were brought back to Manchester and placed on stakes outside the Exchange.

The following morning, Dr Deacon and some of his friends went to see the remains of his son. After being faced with the horrific sight, Deacon removed his hat and bowed his head. Dr Deacon never got to see any of his sons again: Robert was captured and died in a prison in Kendal; after several reprieves Charles was spared the gallows and sentenced to transportation for life to Jamaica, where he died two days after he arrived.

1757 AND 1812

THE SHUDEHILL FIGHT AND THE FOOD RIOT

IN 1756, PEOPLE across the country were struggling to buy basic provisions due to a sharp rise in the cost of food. A series of bad harvests saw the price of wheat and oats double. High food prices, coupled with a seasonal wage, meant that labouring classes faced the serious threat of famine.

By 1757, tension between provision suppliers and the working classes reached boiling point. Throughout the country a series of riots broke out in protest at the soaring costs.

Manchester was hit by two riots in 1757. The first took place in June, when two women grabbed some sacks of potatoes in the market place and began emptying the spuds on the floor in protest. The potatoes were then stolen by other rioters. A cartload of meal was also stolen on its way to market. A shop in Hyde's Cross – now known as the district of Long Millgate – was looted of bread. This time two more women were apprehended and sent to the dungeon. However, the women were not there long before they were broken out by their fellow rioters, who were armed with hammers. Once freed, the women – along with the mob – went back to Hyde's Cross and stole grain, flour and cheese.

The worst of all the skirmishes took place on 15 November, when a 900-strong mob entered the town. The mix of coal miners and weavers had travelled from the neighbouring districts of Ashton-under-Lyne, Saddleworth and Oldham. They travelled to Newton Heath, destroying a corn mill in Clayton, and then into the heart of Manchester. When they reached Shudehill Market, the rioters began to steal a variety of provisions, however their activities were cut short when they were greeted by the High Sheriff and his troops. As the rioters caught sight of the armed men, they began to pelt them with stones, killing one soldier and injuring nine others. In retaliation, the troops fired

Shudehill Market, early twentieth century.

a volley, fatally injuring three men and wounding fifteen. One man, who was not part of the riot, climbed a tree to get a good view of the action but was tragically caught in the crossfire and ended up becoming another victim of the 'Shudehill Fight'. All the injured were transferred to the infirmary. Two hours after the initial skirmish, the rioters returned and attacked a mill owned by a Mr Bramhall. They set fire to several haystacks and damaged the mill owner's home. The mob then waited until nightfall. As darkness fell over the town, they attempted to rescue one of their comrades who was being held in the dungeon on Salford Bridge. Although the daring attempt failed, the governing officials released the man in order to avoid further violence and tension in the town. The man who took the glory for supressing the 'Shudehill Fight' was magistrate John Bradshaw. Bradshaw was born in 1708 in Manchester. At the age of 25 he was given the responsibility of being the commissioner of the peace for the division of Manchester. In 1753, he was promoted to the office of High Sheriff for the county of Lancaster.

In the aftermath of the riots a series of meetings were held and £7,000 was raised to help supply the labouring classes with flour and corn. Similar meetings were held in Liverpool and Stockport, where basic provisions were bought and sold to the workers originally at cost and then at a loss. Although no other riots occurred in Manchester that year, Manchester's history of food rioting was just beginning.

In April 1812, a group of the city's merchants gathered in the Exchange to give thanks to the king for retaining the same ministers in office. The meeting was greeted with anger by the people of Manchester who stormed the building and caused damage inside. After a succession of bad harvests, coupled with rising food prices, the people had had enough of the governing Tory party. A series of food riots followed. On 18 April, rioting lasted for three days. The riot started at Shudehill Market, where traders were demanding 2d for 3lb of potatoes. This was more than the people who were attending the market could afford. A mob that had ascended on the market began picking up the potatoes and launching them at the dealers to drive them off the market. The dealers dropped their prices, but the rioting continued for over an hour and only stopped when the cavalry arrived. Two days later another riot broke out in New Cross which led to the closing of the shops. After this outbreak, farmers and dealers refused to take their produce to market unless that had assurance that they would be safe.

1780–1880

THE COTTON FIRES

A S EARLY AS the eighteenth century, residents across the town were employed in the production of textiles. Spinners and weavers alike were working from makeshift factories in their homes.

Throughout the century, improvements in Manchester's transportation links and advancements in the manufacturing of textiles gave rise to a thriving industry that would see Manchester named 'Cottonopolis'. The famous chimneys that would dominate the town's skyline for the next 150 years originated in the 1780s. The owner of one of these early mills was merchant and inventor Sir Richard Arkwright, whose mill was situated on Miller's Lane, Shudehill. Arkwright was not a native of Manchester, being born to working-class parents in Preston in 1732. The famous mill owner never went to

A Victorian textile factory.

school, but was taught to read and write by his cousin. He began his working life as a barber's assistant, travelling across the region dying hair and socialising with textile workers. It was this that gave him the inspiration to create his first, of many, inventions.

By the 1790s, it was estimated that 70 per cent of the nation's cotton industry could be found in the industrial towns and villages of the North West. By 1815, Manchester's cotton mills were employing over 11,000 men, women and children. A highly flammable substance such as cotton coupled with a flame, such as a lamp, added a deadly hazard to the occupation, and between 1780 and 1880 Manchester witnessed an epidemic of deadly factory fires. One of the worst occurred on a cold Tuesday in January 1801 at the premises of Littlewood and Kirby, which was situated off Oxford Road. The fire started during the day when the mill was full of workers busily spinning cotton. It is believed that the fire started on one of the bottom floors, trapping all the workers on the floors above. The intensity of the fire was so severe that workers began hurling themselves out of the widows and onto the ground below. By the time the fire was extinguished, the factory was in ruins. The death toll was reported at somewhere between eleven and nineteen, with seven people suffering from smoke inhalation and burns.

Only two days after the fire at Littlewood and Kirby, another fire occurred at the factory of a Mr Salsbury in Aldport. The fire started in the evening and quickly spread, until the whole building was alight. All the workers managed to escape, but a woman worker decided to go back into the building to get something. Two men saw her go in and tried to rescue her, however they were unsuccessful and the woman never returned from the building. Her remains were discovered the following day. The fire completely ravaged the building, and not even the walls were left standing.

In 1836, a ferocious fire ripped through the cotton-spinning factory of Faulkner and Owen on Jersey Street, Ancoats. The difference between this fire and the previous fires was that this one appeared to be no accident. By December 1836, the relationship between Mr Faulkner and his workers had broken down and they were on strike. Not wanting to give in to their demands he employed some 'strike-breakers' or 'knob-sticks' as they were otherwise known. Since the turnout started, the strikers had regularly congregated outside the factory and hurled abuse at the new workers. Fearing for his and his new workers' safety, Faulkner had requested the protection of the law and had tried to keep the workers safe by converting a room in the factory for them to live. At 6.30 a.m. on Saturday, 10 December, a fire was discovered in the room where the workers lived. At the time of the fire, half the workers, which consisted of men, women and children, were asleep and the other half were at work in the mill. As the fire took hold, an attempt was made to put out the flames and wake those who were asleep. As the workers fled – mostly wearing nightclothes – the fire spread to the upper part of the factory. By the time the fire service arrived, the whole of the premises was ablaze, only a few bags of cotton were left. Some of the turned-out workers had gathered across from the factory and were cheering as the factory fell in front of them. They then started shouting abuse at the new workers and called for Faulkner to address them. Three hours after the fire started it was finally extinguished, amazingly with no loss of life. Damage to the building was estimated at a staggering £15,000.

In 1842, another fire occurred in one of Manchester's cotton mills. This time it would claim the lives of one man and five children. The fire started at 6 p.m. at the factory of Pooley & Co. on Bradford Street. At the time of the incident, 600 people were working in the mill. The fire was started by one of the machines on the fourth floor. Loose cotton on the machine and on the floor helped to fuel the flames and within minutes the whole floor was ablaze. Several workers tried to put out the flames with buckets of water, but the fire continued to burn. Those that managed to escape waited anxiously in the yard for news of their friends and loved ones. Some of the workers, however, were trapped and their screams and cries for help could be heard by those waiting in the yard. A 14-year-old boy jumped from a fourth-floor window and was killed instantly. When the fire department arrived they entered the building and found the bodies of one man and four children.

1819

THE PETERLOO MASSACRE

ON A HOT August day in 1819, a weaver named Peter Drummond put on his Sunday best, left his house on Strong Street and walked to Mosley Street. Drummond was one of thousands of working-class men, women and children who had travelled into the centre of Manchester hoping to catch a glimpse of radical reformer and 'Orator' Henry Hunt, who was in the city to give a speech on reforming the House of Commons.

Henry Hunt was born in Wiltshire in 1773. Being the son of a wealthy farmer afforded the reformer a private education at a local grammar school and, after ten years of studying, he left school and joined his father in managing the family estates. By 1800 Hunt's father had died and he was in charge of the running of two large estates. The same year, Hunt was found guilty in court of having a dispute with Lord Bruce over the killing of some pheasants. He was sentenced to six weeks' imprisonment. During the trial, Hunt met radical lawyer Henry Clifford, who campaigned for adult suffrage. This was Hunt's introduction to radical politics.

By 1816, Hunt had made a name for himself as a great speaker, travelling across the country giving talks at reform meetings. Such was his popularity that

Peterloo, 1819.

tens of thousands came to listen to him speak. His crowd consisted mostly of working-class men and women who were disgruntled with British politics, which had introduced Corn Laws – which pushed up the price of bread – and had refused to grant them the right to vote. Hunt actively appealed the Corn Laws and campaigned for adult suffrage, making him popular amongst the working classes and sections of the middle classes, but unpopular with the ruling classes, who feared his supporters would try and cause political unrest, similar to that seen in France.

On 16 August 1819, Hunt arrived in Manchester to give a speech on a vacant piece of land on the north side of St Peter's church, known as St Peter's Field. Hunt had campaigned in northern Lancashire towns prior to the rally to ensure that it attracted the sort of crowds that would make the government take notice. It was intended to be one of the largest reform rallies in the country.

Hunt and several other reformers travelled through the city to St Peter's Field in an open landau, which was proceeded by a grand procession of several hundred men, women and children who had travelled from places such as Rochdale, Saddleworth, Oldham, Stockport, Middleton and Mosley. In the hands of the supporters were banners that bore the slogans 'Annul Parliament', 'Universal Suffrage', 'Votes by Ballot' and 'No Corn Laws'.

The party arrived at St Peter's Field at approximately 1 p.m. By now the field was filled as far as the eye could see with supporters. Reports suggest that somewhere in the region of 60,000 people had congregated on the field to hear Hunt speak. Weaver Peter Drummond was one of them. He had missed the travelling procession on Mosley Street, but had made it to St Peter's Field, finding a spot to see the proceedings near the home of the magistrate

A red plaque was erected in 2007 to mark the spot where the Peterloo Massacre took place. The plaque is situation on the corner of the Radisson Blu Edwardian Hotel, Peter Street.

Mr Buxton. While he waited, he saw a man come to the front of the house and say to the waiting constables that the borough reeve and the soldiers were coming. A short time later the Yeomanry Cavalry, supported by police officers with warrants from the magistrates, galloped into the crowd on horseback with their newly sharpened swords drawn. One of the cavalry officers approached Hunt and another reformer named Joseph Johnson, and told them that they had a warrant for their arrest. The pair showed little resistance, and were transferred to the New Bailey Prison. Also apprehended were John Thacker Saxon, Robert Wild, Sarah Hargreaves, Mary Waterworth, George Swift, Eliza Grant and *The Times* reporter John Tyas. While the prisoners were being removed from the field, the cavalry turned their attention to the congregation and an order was given to begin removing the banners. With their swords still drawn, the military men started slashing the banners and stamping them into the ground. By now the crowd were frantic and the scene was chaotic. Trampled bodies lay strewn on the floor. Men, women and children were bleeding from sword wounds. One of those injured was a 71-year-old widow named Alice Kearsley. Alice had travelled from her house on Spital Street to Peter Street to watch the procession. Stood at the side of the Quakers Meeting House, she was minding her own business when one of the cavalry hit her with their sword on the back of the head, knocking her to the floor. The force of the blow was that strong that it nearly sliced her ear clean off! Luckily for Alice, her ear was saved, but it would never be in the same place again.

In total fifteen people were killed on that bloody day in Manchester, with hundreds more being injured. One of the fatalities was a man named John Lee, who had fought at the Battle of Waterloo. The national press had mixed reactions to the event now known as the Peterloo Massacre – named after the Battle of Waterloo. Some labelled the actions of the cavalry as heroic, saving the city from the unruly radicals. However, the overwhelming feeling was one of horror and disgust, and a request was made to get individual members of the cavalry arrested and charged with manslaughter.

1824–1828

THE RESURRECTIONISTS

ENSHROUDED BY THE smog and darkness of the night, two well-dressed men from London and Liverpool named William Johnson and William Harrison were sat in their office on Back King Street. As soon as the lights went out over the town, the two men loaded their gig with tools and drove through the winding streets, keeping out of sight of the local authorities. The men were on their way to the Catholic Granby Row burial ground. Once there, they made sure that that no one was watching. When they were content that they were alone, they reached in the gig for a spade and began digging up a recently occupied grave. Once the men had unearthed the coffin, they prized it open and removed the corpse, placing it into the back of the gig. The men then returned the empty coffin to the grave and recovered it up with earth. They then made their way out of the burial ground and back to their office. Johnson and Harrison were body snatchers or, to coin another phrase, 'resurrection men'.

Throughout January and early February 1824 the men made several trips to various burial grounds and church-yards, each time returning with a body. Their criminal behaviour could well have carried on had their actions not aroused suspicion from their inquisitive neighbours.

After seeing the men coming and going at all hours of the night and carrying packing cases, the neighbours thought that the men were committing robberies and contacted Constable Lavender. Lavender arrived the following day with two of his finest beagles and began to search the offices. To the horror of all at the scene – except Johnson and Harrison – stuffed inside one of the packing bags were two bodies. After the discovery was made, the two men confessed that in the other bags were also bodies that were due to be sent to individuals in London. The men were apprehended on the spot and the hunt then began to find out who the bodies were. Advertisements were placed in the local paper that stated that the bodies would be on display at the George Inn, for one day. Members of the public who had recently buried friends or relatives then applied for tickets to view the bodies. After a full day of viewing was complete the bodies were identified as 74-year-old Edward Hore, 60-year-old Edward Gowry, 49-year-old Catherine Martin, 27-year-old Mary Dunn, 14-year-old Judith Hamilton and 6-year-old Mary Smith. That evening all of the bodies were placed back into their original coffins and re-interred into the ground. The men were later tried and sentenced to fifteen months in Lancaster Castle.

The case of Johnson and Harrison was not the only body snatching incident in Manchester that year. In June 1824, a failed attempt was made to steal a freshly buried body from one of the churchyards. Luckily, the church sexton was alerted that the theft might take place, so he employed two armed men to sit inside the chapel and watch the grave. His suspicions were soon proved right when, sometime after midnight, four men arrived. Two men headed over

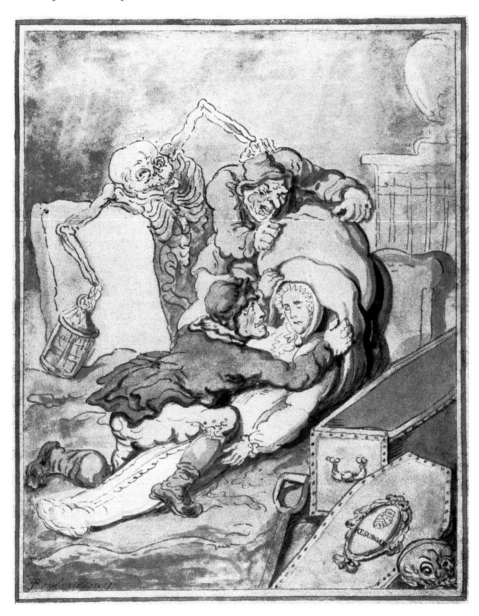

Body snatching in the eighteenth century.

THE ANATOMIST OVERTAKEN by the WATCH :- CARRYING OFF MISS W– in a HAMPER

Body snatching proved a lucrative business in the early nineteenth century.

to the grave and began removing the earth. The two armed men kept watch. Within fifteen minutes, 6ft of earth had been removed. Fearing that the 'resurrection men' were ready to take the body, one of the armed men let out a warning shot. This was enough to scare the men, who gathered their belongings and fled as fast as their feet could carry them.

One body which was not so lucky was that of Mary Howcroft, whose corpse was snatched from the Quaker Burial Ground at Jackson's Row. The perpetrator was a man named John Massey, who lived in a house opposite the burial ground. On the night of 2 May 1828, Massey and three other men went to the grave of Mrs Howcroft and removed her body. The men then placed it in a trunk and took it back to Massey's house before transferring it to a horse and cart and taking it to the Star Coach office. A worker at the office became concerned about what was in the trunk and forced it open. To his horror, inside was the body of Mary Howcroft. Massey was later tried and found guilty of body snatching. He was sentenced to three months' imprisonment.

Body snatching was a lucrative business in the early nineteenth century, especially in towns that had anatomy schools. One corpse could earn a body snatcher or 'resurrectionist' as much as £10. Manchester's leading figure in anatomy during this time was Dr Joseph Jordan, who ran his own anatomy school on Bridge Street. It was reported that not one of his students sent to the Royal College of Surgeons ever failed in anatomy. However, Jordan and his students faced a real dilemma.

They were expected to have knowledge and understanding of the workings of the human body, however before the passing of the Anatomy Act 1832 they were only permitted to dissect bodies of executed prisoners. As the amount of anatomy schools grew in the 1820s, the demand outweighed the supply and there was a real shortage of bodies. The need for bodies was further exacerbated in Manchester when, in 1824, Thomas Turner opened a second anatomy school in Pine Street. The two schools later combined and became the Royal Manchester School of Medicine and Surgery.

Joseph Jordan regularly spoke about the difficulty of obtaining cadavers and admitted in one lecture that he and his students stole bodies themselves. During his early career, ten or twelve bodies were sent to him packed in barrels. Due to the carelessness of the courier, word soon spread about the contents of the barrels and Jordan was faced with an angry mob outside his house at Bridge Street, who smashed all of his windows and frightened him to the point that he did not retreat from his house for several days.

After the Anatomy Act 1832 was introduced, bodies became much easier to obtain because people could now willingly leave their body to science. The Act saw the illegal trade of the resurrection men eventually diminish and body snatchers had to find another way to make their fortune.

1832

THE HEADLESS BOY

ON THURSDAY, 30 AUGUST 1832, the father of 3-year-old John Brogan rushed to the home of Mr Whitelegg to seek medical help for his sick son. The Brogan family lived in a small house on Silk Street, which was just off Oldham Road. With Manchester in the grip of a cholera epidemic, the family feared that the young boy was suffering from the dreaded disease.

Whitelegg, who was the local surgeon, arrived at the house in the afternoon and gave the sick child the usual remedies, which all failed to improve his condition. The doctor then took the decision to admit Brogan to Swan Street Hospital. The young boy arrived at the hospital on Friday afternoon, his condition now critical. Surgeons Gaskell, Lynch and a nurse looked after him until he passed away on the Friday evening. His body was then removed and placed in the dead house (morgue) until his funeral could be arranged. The family applied to the Board of Health for a coffin, which was delivered the following morning. However, when it arrived it was too small. A request was then made for another one, which would not arrive until the Saturday evening, meaning that he could not be buried until the Sunday morning. On the Saturday afternoon, the young boy's grandfather went to see the body to pay his last respects and arrange the funeral.

At some point during Saturday evening / Sunday morning, it was believed that Robert Oldham, who was employed as a dispenser of medicines at the hospital, severed the head from the body. The horrendous incident would have gone unnoticed had it not been for the keen eye of the child's grandfather who noticed at the funeral that his grandson's coffin did not have a name on it. Fearing that something was amiss, the man insisted on seeing the body of his grandson. The coffin was then opened, and, to the horror of all those present, the head was missing and had been replaced by a brick! Further, the coffin was then closed and placed in a public grave at the cholera burial ground, behind the workhouse. After the young boy had been buried, the grandfather returned home and told his neighbours what had happened. Outraged, a mob gathered and marched to the cemetery. When the cemetery gates opened for another funeral, the mob stormed through and went to the grave of John Brogan. His coffin was then removed from the freshly laid grave and opened. Brogan's grandfather immediately reached down and picked up the body of his grandson and began cradling him in his arms.

By now the anger of the waiting crowd was directed at the treatment of cholera victims by the governing officials. Three of the crowd – Burke, Gibson and Pugh – turned to Brogan's grandfather and gently took the body from his arms and placed it back in the coffin. The men then picked up the coffin and placed it on their shoulders. The men and the mob then marched towards New Cross, with shouts of 'Burn the hospital' echoing from the crowd. When they reached New Cross they were met by more supporters, which, according to reports, numbered between 3,000 and 4,000 people. As the mob reached the hospital, the crowd split into two groups, with one party staying at the hospital and the other departing towards the city centre with the coffin.

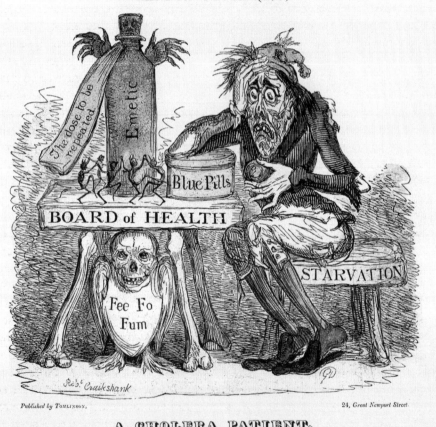

A cholera patient experimenting with remedies, a dig at the Board of Health.

By 6.30 p.m., the crowd at the hospital had forced their way through the hospital gates and had began to demolish the building. Windows were smashed, and chairs, tables and other furniture were broken in the yard and then hurled into the street. By now the police at Shudehill had been told of the riot and were en-route. Not fully understanding the scale of the disturbance, the police force sent a total of twenty officers, which was not enough to cope with the angry mob. After seeing the size of the crowd, reinforcements were sent for. On their arrival the police set upon the angry mob, capturing the thirteen ringleaders. However, the mob only calmed down and dispersed when the Revd Hearne from St Patrick's church arrived and appealed for peace. Shortly before 7 p.m., the priest stood in front of the hospital gates and explained to the waiting crowd that the whole incident was the fault of a man who had gone against the wishes of the hospital and the incident would be passed to the

A sketch of Market Street from Piccadilly. This is where the young boy's body was carried by the mob.

Board of Health. The mob listened and then dispersed shortly before 8 p.m.

While the attack on the hospital was taking place, the group carrying the coffin were still marching. They had travelled down Oldham Street to Piccadilly. Whilst on their journey, they began collecting money from interested bystanders who wished to catch a glimpse of the headless child. As the procession reached Piccadilly they were met a group of special constables who seized the coffin and transferred it to the Town Hall. The devastated family of the child remained at home until the day's events had subsided.

A surgeon from the hospital and the Revd Hearne managed to track down the young boy's head at the lodging house of Robert Oldham. Upon making the discovery, Hearne wrapped the body part in his handkerchief and took it to the Town Hall, where the surgeon reattached it to the body. The following day, a funeral was held at St Patrick's church and the child's body was interred in the burial ground attached to the church. Although a warrant was issued for the arrest of Robert Oldham, he never faced trial. It is believed that he fled the country before he could be caught.

A depiction of Brogan's grave.

1843

THE SOLDIERS
v THE POLICE

O N A WARM May evening in 1843, soldiers from the 15th Regiment were enjoying a drink at a beerhouse on Bengal Street, Ancoats. After hours of drinking and cavorting, two of the men began arguing over the attempted repeal of the union. The argument soon got heated and the men ended up shouting at each other in the street. Two passing police officers caught the soldiers getting ready for a fight. Without a moment's hesitation the officers intervened and attempted to separate and detain the drunken men. Several of the soldiers' comrades – who were inside the beerhouse – rushed outside and began attacking the officers and, fearing for their safety, the officers fled back to their base at Oldham Street Police Station.

The following morning, Super-intendent Stephenson and Sub-Inspector O'Neil ordered their officers to arrest the offenders at their barracks on Tib Street. The soldiers were apprehended and ordered to appear at the magistrates the following day. After hearing all the evidence, the soldiers were fined 20s for the fracas. However, not all of the soldiers could pay the fine, which

meant that they faced a one-month stay at the New Bailey Prison. When word of the fines and sentences got back to the barracks, the men were furious and vowed to take revenge.

Later that evening, Superintendent Stephenson of B Division got word that forty soldiers and a mob were heading up Oldham Road to the police station. Stephenson ordered his men to go and observe what was happening. When the officers arrived, they were met by an angry crowd. The mob appeared to be armed with stones, sticks, batons, pieces of wood with spikes on them and canes.

As the mob reached Oldham Street Police Station, they began to congregate outside, shouting and jeering. A few of the soldiers and the mob then attempted to force their way into the station by charging at the door. When this proved unsuccessful, they began to break all the windows. Once there was no glass left in the window frames, the mob retreated. Fearing another attack was imminent, the superintendent put a request out for more officers, which was met with twenty-five extra men. No sooner had the extra officers arrived than they were greeted by the angry crowd – which

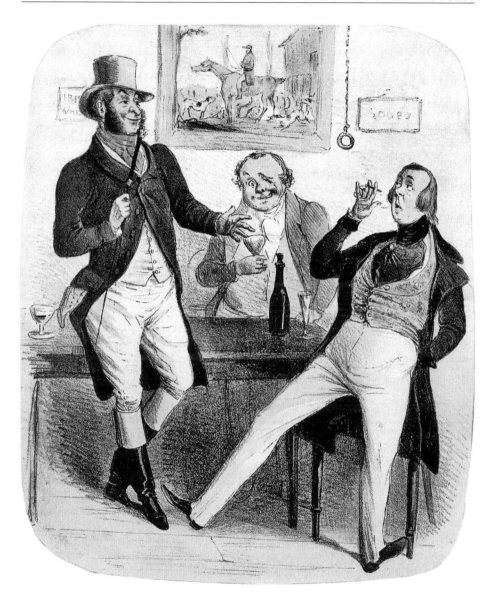

A depiction of the off-duty soldiers enjoying a drink.

had now grown in size and which had returned for a second attack. The riot lasted for several minutes. When the doors were clear, several officers attempted to leave the station and apprehend some of the mob. Ten were eventually caught, however the vast majority of the crowd disappeared into the night. A police officer was ordered by the superintendent to make his was to the army barracks to seek help from the rebels' sergeant. The sergeant stated that he could not leave the barracks and order the men back, however he would get a message to them telling them to return to base.

While the officers of the Oldham Street Station were attempting to fix the damage to their station and apprehend those responsible, the angry mob had moved on to their next target, Kirby Street Police Station in New Islington. When the soldiers and the mob arrived at Kirby Street, they faced an unprepared station. The mob was able to get through the main doors and attack the station officers. The Inspector was kicked to the floor and beaten. An officer named Burgess was so badly assaulted that he was transferred to the Royal Infirmary, where it was hoped that he would recover.

By 6.15 p.m., a message had been sent to the officers at Oldham Street that the Kirby station was under attack. The officers – twenty in total – rushed from Oldham Street and began to chase the rioters down Pollard Street, Great Ancoats Street, New Cross, Spear Street, Deansgate and Port Street. Five soldiers, who had hidden in a coal yard, were cornered by the officers and apprehended. Another soldier, who was hiding in an egg shop, was also caught.

On Wednesday, 24 May, a number of soldiers and civilians were brought up in front of the Borough Court. William Gill, William Woolbridge, John Vernon, Edward Holmes, Michael Higgins, Robert Scott, Charles Gull, Patrick McDonald, Edward Woodhouse, Thomas Vaughan,

New Bailey Prison, Salford, 1832.

John Connor, James Webster, Charles Meehan, John Beeston, James Smith, Charlotte Long, William Harding, Thomas Bell, Joseph Pepper, Mary Lomas, a boy named William King, Robert Garlick, John Hope, John McCale, James Bolan and Ann Millington, all faced trial.

After a long day of hearing evidence from both sides, some of the accused were acquitted, whereas others faced a hefty fine ranging from £15 to £20. Thirteen of the accused – those whom it was deemed committed acts of violence – were apprehended to appear at the next quarter sessions on a charge of riot and assault.

On 23 June 1843, the trial was held at the quarter sessions in Manchester. After hearing all the evidence and personal testimonials, two of the men were acquitted, however the rest were found guilty. Nine of the men were sentenced to twelve months' hard labour at Lancaster Castle. The remaining two men were ordered to serve the same sentence at New Bailey Prison, Salford.

1839–1848

THE HIGHWAY ROBBERS

SOMETIME IN THE morning of 20 April 1839, Ralph Bowyer left his employment at John Howard & Co. in Hyde and walked to Manchester. Bowyer was a trusted employee of the cotton spinners and manufacturers, who gave him the job of walking into Manchester every Saturday to collect the staff's wages from the bank.

That morning started no differently than any other Saturday. Bowyer walked to Manchester, went to the bank and collected 400 sovereigns and £250 in notes. He placed the sovereigns in a bag around his neck, the notes in his pocket and headed back to work.

Bowyer was making his way along Hyde Road when, at about 11 a.m., he decided to stop and pick some watercress from a field. Three men – who he thought were workmen – approached him and told him that there was more watercress down the next lane and they would show him where it was. Thanking them for their kindness, he followed the men, who pointed to a ditch where they claimed the plant was growing. As he bent over to find the cress, Bowyer was

Cheetham Hill Road, c. 1920.

hit over the head with a large stone, knocking him to the floor. The wounded man began to shout 'Murder! Murder!' His attempt to get help only angered the men, who began hitting him with stones. To stop him from shouting, the two men attempted to stuff a handkerchief in his mouth. One of the men then reached for the bag around his neck and pulled it with such force that it snapped off. Once they had the sovereigns the robbers fled, without taking the notes that were still concealed in Bowyer's pocket.

As Bowyer came around, he noticed that he was bleeding heavily from wounds to his head. Desperate to get help, he staggered to Gorton. As he arrived in the village, some of the local residents came out of their houses to help him. A group of local men went off in search of the culprits. A farmer found one of the men hiding in a hedge and managed to apprehend him. The other man was later caught by Manchester police and placed in custody at a lock-up in Gorton. The culprit was found with blood on his shirt, his trousers and on his wrists. While in custody the man

The entrance to Heaton Park, c. 1910.

revealed that his name was Alexander Mee. He claimed that he lived at St James's Court, Camp Street, Manchester, and was employed as a dyer.

Mee, along with two other men, was later brought up at the New Bailey. Bowyer testified that Mee was the one that had hit him, however he did not recognise the other men, so they were released. Twenty-three-year-old Mee, on the other hand, was committed for trial at the next assizes. He was tried at the assize on 13 August and after hearing all the evidence the jury found him guilty and sentenced to him to ten years' transportation.

No less that a decade after Mee was convicted, another daring highway robbery took place in the district of Manchester. The victim was the Revd Nicholas Germon, high master of the Manchester Grammar School. The events began on Saturday, 15 January 1848, when Germon was riding with his wife and two children in an open-top carriage along Cheetham Hill Road. After travelling for some time, Germon, his wife and daughter decided to get out and walk, letting his son ride on. As they reached Heaton Park, two men named Daniel O'Brien and Michael Connolly lay in wait for them to pass. When Germon and his wife were in touching distance, the men jumped out and one of them pointed a large pistol at Germon's chest while the other went behind him and pointed a gun in his back. The men demanded the couple's watches and money or they would shoot. Mrs Germon handed over her watch and then fled to a passing carriage shouting 'Murder!'

Flustered, the men started to lose their patience and their threats became more severe. Fearing for his life, Germon handed over his watch and purse and the men fled down Middleton Road, jumped over a hedge and into the fields towards Blackley. The robbers only got a short distance when they decided to change direction and head towards Crumpsall. Later that day, the police raided a pub and apprehended a known criminal on suspicion of robbery, however after a negative identity parade, the man was released.

After further investigations a raid was made on 8 February at a beer-house in Shudehill. The police now had their men. Twenty-seven-year old O'Brien and 26-year-old Connolly were taken into custody on suspicion of theft. After another identity parade, Germon confirmed that O'Brien and Connolly were the robbers. After a trial at the assize on 23 March 1848, both men were found guilty by jury and sentenced to fifteen years' transportation.

The men started their transportation to Western Australia on 17 November 1852 on board the ship *Dudbrook*. The journey would take between four and six months. Conditions on board the ships were dismal, with many convicts dying before they reached their destination. Between 1787 and 1868 over 150,000 convicts were sent to Australia. They included men, women and children. After serving their sentence, many of the convicts found employment and settled in Australia. There is no evidence to suggest that O'Brien or Connolly ever returned to Manchester.

1853–1858

THE DANGERS OF PROGRESS

ON 15 SEPTEMBER 1830, the railway finally came to Manchester. Thousands turned out at Liverpool Road Station to celebrate its arrival. The first line connected Manchester to the port town of Liverpool. By the 1850s, the rail network had increased significantly, connecting the city to the Midlands, Cheshire, Lancashire and Yorkshire. This new form of transportation brought joy and danger for those living in the industrial city.

The new railway lacked any proper health and safety features.

In 1819, the All England Eleven cricketer Thomas Hunt was born in Chesterfield. Hunt was a coachman by trade, however between 1844 and 1858 he played professional cricket. He started his cricket career in Chesterfield before moving to Sheffield and later Manchester. Hunt was a talented cricketer, being labelled 'the best single wicket player in Britain' at the time. Hunt's good looks combined with his ability earned him an allegiance of fans.

In 1851, Hunt and his family moved to Manchester to play for the Manchester Cricket Club. Hunt, his wife Elizabeth and two children settled in Old Trafford. It was during his time here that he was asked to play for the All England Eleven.

On Saturday, 11 September 1858, Hunt had an away game with the All England Eleven in Rochdale. He travelled to the railway station with his wife by omnibus. As they reached the station the pair said their goodbyes and agreed to meet when Hunt returned to Manchester on the 7 p.m. train later that evening.

Hunt arrived at the cricket ground shortly after 10 a.m. and at 10.45 a.m. the first over started. The game was played in front of a packed crowd and lasted until the early evening.

Once the game was finished, Hunt collected his wage of £20 and gathered up his belongings. He was invited to a dinner at the Wellington Hotel, Rochdale, to celebrate the team playing in the town, but declined, wishing to make sure that he was on the 7 p.m.

train back to Manchester to meet his wife. The cricketer and a porter named John Wild then set off to the station. Hunt and Wild decided to take a shortcut to the station by walking along the track that backed on to the cricket pavilion. The men entered the track and started walking when Wild heard a whistling sound coming from behind them. He immediately turned around and discovered that the sound was that of a train: the 6.50 train from Rochdale to Manchester.

Wild shouted to Hunt, who was walking ahead, however he didn't hear him and was hit by the buffer which knocked him to the ground. His hands and legs were resting on the tracks and as the train passed it sliced off his hands and legs at the thighs.

As the star cricketer lay injured on the tracks, spectators from the match and the stationmaster rushed to his aid. He was immediately transferred by cart to the Fleece Inn, which was next to the station, and a surgeon was called for. The surgeon worked on him for an hour and then told the waiting public that Hunt was dying. A vicar was then sent for and a telegram was sent to his wife. Elizabeth got on the first available train to Rochdale. However, by the time she arrived her husband had died, sadly passing away just five minutes before she arrived. After his death, collections were made across the city for his wife and children, and better safety procedures were put in place to stop people getting onto the track, owned by the Lancashire and Yorkshire Railway. The inquest revealed that there was nothing that the driver could have done to prevent the accident.

Since its opening in 1839, the line from Manchester to Yorkshire had witnessed its fair share of accidents, some of which involved pedestrians on the track and others involving

The Royal Infirmary, Piccadilly, c. 1906.

train collisions. One of the latter occurred on a cold, snowy day in December 1853. The events began shortly after 9.30 a.m. at Victoria Station. The next train out of the station that day was the 9.40 Yorkshire train, which stopped at Miles Platting, Newton Heath and Rochdale, before passing into Yorkshire. Five minutes after the Yorkshire train, the Oldham Express was scheduled to depart from the same station. The Oldham was a direct train and made no stops. On the day in question, the Yorkshire train left Manchester as scheduled. The Oldham train was slightly delayed due to a problem at Middleton. The driver of the train somehow managed to make up some distance with the train in front, which ended with disastrous consequences at Newton Heath Station. As the Oldham train approached the station, the stationmaster signalled for the train to slow down because the Yorkshire train was still at the platform. The driver failed to see the warning sign because he had already driven past the signal post and subsequently crashed into the back of the Yorkshire train at a speed of 15mph. The crash damaged the rear second-class carriage of the train. Such was the force that the guard and the passengers were thrown out onto the track. The scene at the station was one of chaos. The stationmaster, his wife and local residents rushed to help the victims. An 18 year old from Huddersfield named Jane Sykes was one of the first victims to be helped.

She had been travelling with her grandmother when the train crashed. Sykes was taken into the station house, where the wife of the stationmaster took care of her. Sadly, the young woman could not be saved. She let out a few cries and then died in the arms of the stationmaster's wife. The young lady's grandmother was also taken to the station house. She had suffered concussion after hitting her head. After coming round she was transferred to the Royal Infirmary. Several other passengers were also injured, suffering from loss of limbs, broken bones, cuts and shock. Luckily, two surgeons were in the area and performed first aid on some of the injured. Had it not been for the two doctors, it is likely that the death toll would have been higher.

Accompanied by one of the surgeons, the thirteen people who were seriously injured were placed on the Bradford train back to Manchester to get medical assistance. The body of the only fatality, Jane Sykes, was later removed from the station house and placed in the Duke of York Inn awaiting an inquest. Such was the grim curiosity of the locals that the landlady had to physically stop sightseers from peering at the body. It transpired at the inquest that Sykes and her grandmother had left Preston that morning for Huddersfield. The women had been told in Bolton to get on the Manchester train by a porter, however this was the wrong train and tragically the women should never have been on it.

1858

THE QUACK DOCTORS

DURING THE SUMMER of 1857, life was good for 27-year-old Margaret Belborough – well, as good as it could be living under the smoke-filled chimneys of the city's Victorian industrial landscape. Margaret was healthy, she had a roof over her head and she was in employment, working in her uncle's teashop in Hulme. However, by the winter of 1857, things began to change for the worse. Her uncle, Joshua Bilcliffe, had to sell his teashop and Margaret was made unemployed. With no job and no income, Margaret moved to Todcaster to get work. She had not been in Todcaster long when she received a message from her uncle to say that he was opening a beerhouse called the General Havelock on Streford New Road. With the promise of employment, Margaret moved back to Manchester.

While Margaret was settling back into life in Manchester, the city was also welcoming another new resident by the name of Carl Stadtmüller. Stadtmüller, a doctor, had come to Manchester from Germany to work with a fellow German doctor by the name of Auguste Wilhelm. Wilhelm kept premises on Deansgate and later on Bury New Road, Strangeways. Wilhelm was a man of questionable character. He had arrived

Deansgate, c. 1900.

in Manchester from Halifax with his wife and children sometime after 1853. By September 1858, Wilhelm and his new assistant Stadtmüller had gained a new patient, Margaret Belborough. Margaret was in trouble. She was pregnant and the father of the child wanted nothing to do with her or the baby. At first Margaret sent a note to Wilhelm with a payment for drugs that would procure an abortion. Over the space of a month, a messenger delivered six notes with money in return for medicines. However, by the end of September, Margaret was concerned that she was still pregnant and it was starting to show.

On Sunday, 25 September, Margaret decided to pay a visit to Wilhelm's home at Strangeways. She arrived shortly after 2 p.m. and was greeted by Wilhelm, his wife and Stadtmüller. Wilhelm and his wife took her into a room with a bed and told her to lie on her back. The doctor then turned to his assistant and told him that he was going to carry out an abortion and asked him what tools he had. He then picked up an instrument that is normally used to pierce the skull of children during post-mortems, and carried out the abortion. The pain from the procedure was so severe that Mrs Wilhelm had to hold Margaret down, bruising her arm in the process. A young girl, who was passing the shop at the time, could hear Margaret's screams from the street. As soon as it was dark, Margaret, supported by Mrs Wilhelm, was placed in a cab and the ladies travelled back to Margaret's house. The young woman was then helped into bed. The following day Margaret's pain was worse and her condition appeared to be deteriorating. Her uncle, Joshua Bilcliffe, tried to go and get the family doctor, but Margaret refused, saying she would only see Wilhelm. Wilhelm and Stadtmüller visited Margaret several times that day. They gave her leeches and powders, however her condition did not improve. Margaret's uncle sent for a family friend named Mrs Wainwright and it was to her that Margaret confessed that she had been to Wilhelm to hide her 'shame'.

A rather romantic picture of Kirkdale Prison, 1819.

The following day, Margaret was close to death. Wilhelm and Stadtmüller arrived in her room and began to empty all the medicine bottles they had prescribed down the sink. By now the pain was unbearable. As soon as the doctors left, her uncle fetched the family doctor. When Dr Wilson arrived he examined Margaret and discovered that she had suffered a partial abortion and was now showing signs of blood poisoning. Dr Wilson stayed with Margaret until she passed away. He then marched to the surgery of Wilhelm and Stadtmüller and accused them of endeavouring to carry out an abortion. The pair denied the charge against them and stated that the woman had done it to herself. Wilhelm argued that he had never met the woman prior to when she turned up at his surgery on the Sunday. Not believing their story, Dr Wilson went to the police. After a thorough search, the instruments that were used in the abortion were found in the possession of Stadtmüller. Both men were then apprehended and sent to trial. Stadtmüller had never been in trouble with the police before in England, and for a man who only spoke basic English, the thought of standing trial must have been a daunting prospect. For Wilhelm though it was not the first time he had appeared in an English court. In 1853, while working in Halifax, a young lady and a respectable gentleman approached Wilhelm and asked him if he would carry out an abortion. The couple were in a relationship when the child was conceived, however they were not married and nor did they have any plans to marry. Wilhelm gave the woman some medicine but it did not work. She then went to his surgery where she testified that Wilhelm attempted to abort the foetus – something that he later denied, stating that she was examined because she had a vaginal disease. At a subsequent trial, even though the woman herself testified against Wilhelm, he was found not guilty after a long deliberation.

In the trial of 1858, Wilhelm would not be so lucky. His assistant, Stadtmüller, was acquitted and acted as a witness for the prosecution. The assistant confirmed that Wilhelm had carrried out an abortion on Margaret Belborough. After hearing all the evidence, the judge stated that if the jury believed that Wilhelm had used an instrument or medicine for unlawful reasons and death occurred, he should be found guilty of murder, even though he may not have meant to kill the person. After a short deliberation the jury found Wilhelm guilty of murder and he was sentenced to death. The doctor pleaded with the judge to spare him on the grounds that his wife and child would face a life of poverty without him. His plea was ignored and he was transferred to Kirkdale Prison. Two weeks after the trial the Home Office wrote to the Governor of the prison and respited the sentence of death.

1866–1880

'TILL DEATH DO US PART'

ON CHRISTMAS EVE 1866, a shoemaker named William Cassidy married his sweetheart, an Irish girl named Rose Ann Hogg. The Hoggs had arrived in Manchester shortly after the potato famine. The family resided just off the Rochdale Road, and it was while living here that Rose met William, who lived just a few streets away.

After the couple wed, they moved to their own home at Red Bank. Following the birth of their third child they left Red Bank and settled in a two-up two-down on Susan Street. By 1879, they had five children. William was now employed in the shoe trade and Rose was working as a machinist.

By now cracks were starting to appear in their marriage. Both Rose and William liked a drink, which would often cause the pair to argue and fight. In the months leading up to November 1879, the arguments became more frequent and intense, with William making threats to kill his wife.

The Bottle, by George Cruikshank, 1847.

On 10 November, Rose went to bed as normal. William was not in at the time – he was at the local pub, the Nelson Inn. He arrived home sometime around 1.00 a.m. While Rose was sleeping, William took a paraffin lamp that was in the bedroom and poured the oil all over her bed. He then set fire to it. Within seconds the bed was engulfed in flames. Rose woke and caught sight of her husband walking out of the bedroom and down the stairs. She managed to get up and stumble to the bedroom door. A police officer that was walking past at the time saw flames coming from the bedroom window and attempted to gain entry to the house. After being let in by the son of the couple, he dashed upstairs and saw Rose on the landing with severe burns. He immediately got her transferred to the hospital, where she died two days later, but not before she told the police that her husband had done this; he had tried to kill her.

William was arrested a short time later and faced a subsequent trial at the assize. After hearing all the evidence, he was found guilty and sentenced to death.

He was executed at Strangeways Prison on 17 February 1880, shortly after 8 a.m. William Marwood, the executioner, met Cassidy in the morning and stated that he seemed very calm and showed no remorse. At 8.10 a.m. the black flag was raised over the prison. The Governor refused to allow reporters into the execution, however it was stated that the executioner used a drop of 9ft 6in, which was one of the biggest drops ever used. The drop was so long that it nearly ripped Cassidy's head from his body.

The Assize Courts, Manchester, 1907.

As shocking at this murder may seem, it was not uncommon. In Manchester there was a real epidemic of spousal murders during the nineteenth century, and nearly all involved the 'demon drink'.

A little over eight months after the execution of Cassidy, a woman in the district of Rochdale Road was killed by her husband. The victim was in her early twenties and named Bridget Chorlton. Bridget and her husband John liked to drink. It was said that while John was at work, his wife would spend money on drink, and when he was home they would drink together. The couple both had a history of violence, however it was Bridget who always came worse off. In 1879, John beat his wife so badly that she was admitted to the infirmary, where she spent several days recovering. A warrant was issued for his arrest, however he went on the run and was never caught. When he eventually returned to Manchester, he managed to convince his wife not to prosecute him and the couple rekindled their relationship.

By September 1880, the couple were arguing again and John was back to his violent ways. On the evening of 28 September, John was in the local beerhouse complaining about his wife. He stated that unless she changed her ways and stopped drinking he would kill her and hang for it. John arrived home at 10.30 p.m. Sometime between then and 11.30 p.m. the couple got into an argument. It is alleged that during the quarrel John picked up some tongs and hit Bridget across the face with them several times, killing her instantly. The coroner revealed at the inquest that it was one of the most brutal murders that he had ever come across. Chorlton was sent to the assize charged with his wife's murder.

His trial began on 3 November 1880. His defence tried to claim that his wife fell out of bed while drunk, however this was contested by the prosecution. After hearing all the evidence, the jury acquitted him of murder but found him guilty of the lesser charge of manslaughter. He was sentenced to penal servitude for life.

1866

THE MANCHESTER ROBBERY

IN MAY 1866, at the Crystal Fountain beerhouse in Lambeth, London, four men named Charles Leeson, Charles Batt, William Douglas and Thomas Henry Douglas were conducting a meeting. The four men were in the midst of planning one of the most audacious robberies of their generation. The location was Manchester. The target would be the Stamp Office, where the gang would help themselves to over £12,000-worth of government stamps, receipts and foreign money. The date of the robbery would be 27 May.

The men arrived in the city sometime on 24 May 1866 to organise their attack. The would-be thieves studied plans of the Stamp Office and the surrounding buildings so they could work out the best way to enter and leave the building.

Sometime on 26 May the men went to the back of the building – which was on Cross Street – and made their entrance through an alleyway which was shared with other offices. Doing their best not to be seen, the men then waited until everyone had left the building. By lunchtime, two men were still inside the premises, a photographer named McLachlan and a porter. It would not be until 6 p.m. that the building would be empty. The men had not planned that it would take so long for everyone to leave

the premises. It was now a race against time to get the job completed and be out before the office staff arrived the following morning.

When the coast was clear, the men entered the offices of Garnett and Horsfalls, who were cotton manufacturers, by breaking the lock on their door. They then gained entry to the warehouse and stole a large quantity of cloth. The men then headed to the rear of the warehouse and down some stairs, which led to a room empty except for a fixed table. The room backed on to the Stamp Office and Robinson Street. The men started to remove the bricks from the wall, which was hidden by the table. The wall was 9in thick and it took some time before a hole was big enough for one man at a time to squeeze through. While one of the men went through the hole, the others carefully sifted through all of the drawers of the Hon. R.E. Howard, who was the distributer of the stamps for Manchester. The thieves read the contents of the drawers, which consisted mostly of letters, and then carefully placed them back in their original position, so it appeared as if they had not been disturbed. They then made their way out of the office and into a passageway that joined the Cross Street lobby. From there the men were able to force open the lock that led to the room where the safe was. The safe was positioned in the corner of the room and next to it was a table. The men quickly moved the table to the centre of the room and laid out the fabric that they had stolen earlier. The safe weighed over 1,500lb and was over 4ft in height, meaning that they couldn't lift it. Instead they decided to tip the safe onto the fabric, which would stop it from making any noise. A hole was then drilled in the top of the safe and markers were placed in the door to keep it open. The men then emptied the contents of the safe into bags and made their escape, leaving behind a large sledgehammer and tools. Their escape plan was just as ambitious as their entrance. They disappeared through a door that they had secured with an iron bar and lock. The thieves even went as far as to put a latch on the door with a piece of string attached, so that when they made their escape they could shut the door from the other side by pulling the string. The men knew that this would slow the police down if they tried to gain entry because they wouldn't be able to open it from their side. The men then took their loot and travelled back to London. The full extent

A portion of the loot (£4,000) was stashed at the luggage office at Euston Station, c. 1900.

of the robbery was not discovered till the following day, which gave the thieves the chance to deposit £4,000 at each of the left luggage offices at Euston Station and Paddington Station. What happened to the rest of the stamps remained a mystery.

After making the discovery on the Monday morning, the Stamp Office issued a reward of £400 for the return of the missing stamps and the apprehension of the criminals. While the police were carrying out their enquiries, Batt and Leeson were attempting to get rid of some of the stamps at the Stamp Office in Somerset House. However, the staff were already on alert for the stolen stamps and called the police. Batt and Leeson were arrested and sent to Manchester to await trial. The Douglas brothers managed to evade capture until September, when they were eventually caught at Doncaster Races. In their possession was a copy of *Wrights Turf Guide*, which was the same paper found at the scene of the robbery.

All four men were tried at the assize on 10 December 1866. At the trial a majority of the evidence was circumstantial. Members of the public came forward that put the four London men in the vicinity of the Stamp Office at the time of the crime. After a trial that lasted two days, all four men were found guilty. Batt was sentenced to ten years' penal servitude. Leeson and the two Douglas brothers were sentenced to fifteen years' penal servitude. The men were then transferred to New Bailey Prison.

By the middle of December, the stamps had still not been found and as the distributer of the stamps, The Hon. R.E. Howard would be held responsible unless they were recovered. The Governor of New Bailey Prison took it upon himself to try and discover where they were being hidden. He summoned Leeson to a meeting and suggested that he should admit where the stash was to ease his conscience. Leeson refused unless it would lead to a reduction in his sentence, however this was declined by the Governor. Leeson suggested that if he could speak to the other three men he might change his mind. After a brief meeting the four robbers agreed to tell Howard where his stamps were. The police, accompanied by the men's wives, then left Manchester by the North-Western express and retrieved the missing stamps.

1872

THE FLOATING BODIES

A **LITTLE BEFORE** midnight on Friday, 12 July 1872, a couple from Ancoats were strolling home after enjoying a night of socialising in the local pub. As they arrived home, the weather took a turn for the worse. Torrential rain would batter the city for the next thirteen hours. Residents stated that it was like a 'water spout had broken out over the city'. Manchester's flood defences were no match for mother nature. One of the worst affected areas were the houses and businesses that were in the vicinity of the River Medlock, which had burst its banks causing severe flooding, but also Manchester's Philip's Park Cemetery. By the Saturday afternoon, the eastern portion of the Roman Catholic section of the cemetery had flooded. The water had ripped through the boundary wall and re-entered the river at Bank Bridge Print Works. Coffins that had been newly laid were washed from their graves and swept away with the flow of water into the city.

For the following three days bodies were recovered from as far away as Castlefield, which was 3 miles from the cemetery. During Saturday and Sunday, fifteen were recovered in the district of the cemetery. Thirty-six were removed from Fairfield Police Station

after they had been deposited there by members of the public and police. Ten were discovered in the River Medlock at Ogden Street. Two were found at a pub in Oxford Road and one at a pub in Knott Mill. In total it was estimated that seventy-six bodies had been washed away. It appeared that they had been buried between the years 1867 and 1869. After a request was sent to the Guardians of the Poor, eighty coffins were provided and the bodies were re-interred in a higher portion of ground in the Roman Catholic part of the cemetery.

The flood of 1872 was the not the first time that this section had been under water. In 1868, a flood defence was built along the riverbank. In 1869, the Catholic community argued that the wall was not adequate enough to protect their section of the cemetery from future flooding, and they were right.

Since the opening of the cemetery in 1866 to the flood in 1872, over 12,000 burials had been conducted in the 8-acre Roman Catholic section of the cemetery. The most popular form of burial was the public grave, which could take as many as twenty coffins.

In the wake of the floods, the Catholic community became increasingly angered by the treatment they had received from the council. Since the cemetery opened, community leaders had argued that of all of the religious denominations they had been given the worst plot of land in the cemetery. However, now they had a point. A local Catholic priest wrote to the *Manchester Guardian* and the Home Secretary stating that a public inquiry by the Home Office was needed to address the failings of the Corporation. Another writer to the *Guardian* suggested that the Catholic community needed a cemetery of their own.

A public inquiry was held at the cemetery on 24 July 1872. In charge of the proceedings was Philip Henry Holland, Burials Inspector for the Home Office. The council was represented by Mayor Booth, City Surveyor Lynde, members of the Cemetery Committee and the Town Clerk, Sir Joseph Heron. On the side of the Catholic community was Canon Cantwell, P. Liptrot, John Gornall and some local Catholic priests and members of the public. Before the meeting started, disagreements were already taking place between the two parties. The Burials Inspector argued that the meeting should take place on neutral ground, whereas John Gornall felt it should be at the Catholic chapel. After a heated debate it was decided the meeting should take place in the 'neutral' dissenters chapel. The result angered members of the public, who shouted, 'We want to be treated as Christians not as barbarians'.

Philip's Park Cemetery, 2016.

The feeling throughout the meeting was one of hostility towards the Burial Inspector and members of the council. Even before the inquiry officially opened, members of the public could be heard shouting angrily. Worried for the safety of council members, the police were called to stop any violence and keep the public in order.

After surveying the damage, the Burials Inspector read the letter that was sent to the Home Secretary. The Home Secretary then stated that he was only interested in the events that happened the night of the flood and how it could be prevented in the future. After a series of heated debates on both sides, the council revealed that they planned to build a new river wall and stop all burials in the low-lying part of the cemetery. The council stated that the cause of the flood was over 20,000 pieces of calico that had been dumped in the Medlock from Wood and Wright's printworks. The calico had travelled down the river and got trapped at the weir, restricting the flow of water, which caused a blockage and directed the water through the cemetery.

Describing the Corporation's version of events as 'beautifully coloured', the Catholic community were not happy about what they had heard at the inquiry. Although burials did stop in the low-lying part of the Catholic cemetery, the Catholic community still felt that they had been treated unfairly by the Corporation. In 1875, just three years after the flood of 1872, the Catholics opened their own cemetery in Moston, 3 miles from Philip's Park. Named St Joseph's, it had an immediate impact on the number of Catholic burials in Philip's Park, which fell dramatically.

1880–1910

THE SCUTTLERS AND THE IKES

IN THE LAST quarter of the nineteenth century the streets of north-east Manchester, Salford, Gorton and Openshaw were overrun by gangs. They were made up of groups of youths who named themselves after the street where they lived. In Manchester there were the Bengal Street Tigers, Grey Mare Boys, Holland Street and Alum Street. They were known as the scuttlers, because they would fight for the honour of their street using makeshift weapons, such as belts and knives. Each gang would fight each other and other areas – gangs in Salford would team up and fight the gangs of Ancoats. By the 1890s scuttler gangs had taken over whole districts of the city and were even operating the doors of some of the town's entertainment venues.

On a cold day in February 1895, people in Manchester were enjoying entertainment at the 'Cas' music hall. The People's Concert Hall – as it was officially known – was on Lower Mosley Street and was a popular destination for working-class men and women. In the venue that night was Richard Beatey, William Norris, Joseph Hewitt, John Green, Christopher Matthews and Robert Edward Brassell. The lads, aged between 17 and 21, were members of a scuttler gang from Salford called the

Adelphi. While the youths were socialising inside, they spotted a rival gang member named John Fallon. The gang walked up to Fallon and without warning stabbed him in the head. Fallon managed to stagger away, while the rest of the gang were thrown out by the management of the hall. Once outside, the gang caught sight of Fallon and reportedly shouted 'come on lads, let's cut him up'. They then began attacking him again. A passer-by named Patrick Hughes tried in vain to stop the attack, and the gang turned their attention on him. Beatey – who was the leader – marched up to Hughes with a penknife in his hand and stabbed him in the head. Joseph Hewitt followed and also stabbed Hughes. Although he was bleeding heavily, Hughes managed to drag himself up and run towards Bale Street. The gang were now in pursuit, and unluckily for Hughes, he fell and the youths caught him. He was stabbed twice in the head and shoulder, and was also kicked and hit with a belt whilst on the ground. He might have lost his life had it not been for the quick actions of two men who were passing and managed to chase the scuttlers off with sticks. Hughes was taken to the Royal Infirmary. When he was well enough, he testified against the scuttlers at a later trial at the assize. After hearing all the evidence, all but John Green were found guilty. The gang were handed heavy sentences in the hope that they would act as a deterrent to other scuttlers. Ringleader Richard Beatey was sentenced to five years' penal servitude. As it was not proved that Brassell had a knife, he was sent to prison with hard labour for eighteen months. Hewitt was given four years penal servitude. Norris, who had already served five years at the *Akbar* reformatory training ship, was sentenced to four years' penal servitude, and Matthews was given an eighteen-month prison sentence with hard labour.

It was not just men that were involved in scuttling; girls were also participants. It was reported that the girls fought with more violence than the boys. In May 1892, four girls were brought up at the City Police Court charged with scuttling. All four were sentenced to one month's imprisonment. One of the girls had a tattoo with the words 'In Loving Remembrance of William Willan'. William Willan was the 'king of the scuttlers', a title given to a scuttler who had proved himself as a leader and fighter. Both Willan and the tattooed girl were part of the Lima Street gang. Willan was not actually dead – or at least not yet. At the time of the girls' arrest, Willan was in a prison cell awaiting execution after having been found guilty of the murder of Peter Kennedy, a member of the rival Bradford Street gang. His execution was due to take place on 31 May, but was postponed after a petition was sent to the Home Secretary. After reading the petition and taking into account the boy's age, the sentence was reduced to penal servitude for life.

Another scuttler who was regularly in trouble with the police was John Moores. Moores, who went by the name 'Pony', operated with his gang in the Hulme district of the city. One evening in September 1899, Pony and his gang were walking down City Road when they started to throw some fish, which was on display in a shop window. A man named William Corlett was crossing over City Road at that moment and came face-to-face with Pony. Without warning or provocation, Pony shouted, 'You take that', and stabbed Corlett in the left side of his chest. With blood dripping from his shirt, the injured man managed to stagger home, and it was only then that he realised he had been stabbed. It was later revealed that if he had not been wearing braces, it was likely that the stab wound would have killed him. After the attack on Corlett, the gang broke several shop windows and stole beer from a beerhouse. They also assaulted another man and threw a bottle at a confectioner.

At the time of this attack in 1899, the scuttler gangs were starting to disappear from the streets. Lads' clubs and the heavy sentences handed out by the authorities all assisted in their demise. However, it would not be long before the 'Ikes' were taking over. Ikes were deemed a lower class than the scuttlers and on the whole lacked the violence. They rarely worked, showed little sign of trying to get employment, and made a life out of crime. The Ikes' dress was distinctive. They would wear bell bottom-style trousers, pointed clogs, a silk neck scarf and a jacket that had buttons grouped in rows of five. Their hair was cut short, however they allowed their fringe to grow long, which would be fixed to the forehead covering an eye.

Jonas Sunmer; a criminal with the traditional 'Ike' haircut.
(© Greater Manchester Police Museum)

1905

THE RIOT FOR THE UNEMPLOYED

IN THE LATE spring of 1867, a bookbinder named John Francis Skevington and his wife Harriet Ann Cobain welcomed their second son into the world. The couple called the boy William Edward. William spent his childhood in a small terrace in Hulme. When he was in his teens, William found employment in the iron industry as a mechanic. In 1890, at the age of 22, he married a local girl named Ada Hutchinson. It was after his marriage to Ada that he became involved in politics, joining the Social Democratic Federation (SDF).

The SDF was founded in 1884 and was Britain's first socialist party. The party was far more radical than any of the other political parties. They believed that to get their point across they would need to get the attention of the public and Westminster. To do this they hosted a series of rallies and demonstrations. Labelled as the 'first Marxist party in Britain' the party campaigned for better housing for the working classes, free and compulsory education for children, free school meals and better treatment of the unemployed from the government.

The party carried out a number of demonstrations in the 1880s in London and Ireland to support the unemployed. The rallies went under the tag line 'A Right to Work'. However, most of these demonstrations ended up in riots, with shops being looted and windows being smashed. Members of the crowd were also arrested for fighting with the police.

By 1896, William was a member of the SDF. He was now running his own successful shop selling groceries and provisions. The shop occupied two buildings and afforded him the luxury of a servant. His position as a shopkeeper and of living in Hulme gave William an insight into what a struggle it was for working-class people to live without employment. Twice he was nominated as a member of the Chorlton Board of Guardians and twice he failed to secure enough votes. In 1902 he received only 290 votes, which was the lowest number of votes out of all of the nominees. However, by 1904 William managed to get elected onto the South Manchester Board of Guardians.

The following year William had worked his way up the ranks of the SDF and was seen as one of the 'leaders' in Manchester. He was also chairman of the Unemployed Committee. In July 1905, William and two other men named Robert McGregor and Charles Steadman called for a series of demonstrations to be held in Manchester. The meetings would be held at Albert Square and would be in protest against the Conservatives' treatment of the unemployed. The largest meeting was planned for 31 July. It was scheduled that the men would address the crowd at Albert Square and then they would walk to Piccadilly where another meeting would take place.

On the day of the meeting, a crowd of roughly 500 had gathered in Albert Square. At 1 p.m. William addressed the waiting people. He started by stating that he hoped the Employment Bill would be passed, however something needed to be done to 'force the hand of the government'. The next speaker was a man named Arthur Smith, who urged the crowd to form an army and demand their rights. More speakers followed, which further ignited the passions of the crowd. At 2 p.m., William and Smith removed the banner that read 'We Demand the Unemployment Bill!' The crowd then left Albert Square

Albert Square in 1923: the venue for many radical meetings.

and marched down Cross Street, up Market Street and towards Piccadilly. As the protest reached Market Street, they were joined by the police, who attempted to keep the party moving and stop them from blocking the road. However, a skirmish quickly escalated between the protesters and the police. The police with their batons drawn started fighting with the crowd. Fists were flying in both directions and there were multiple injuries on both sides. William, Arthur Smith and Robert McGregor were arrested at the scene and transferred to the Town Hall, where they were charged and then released on bail. The rest of the crowd were dispersed by the police. The actions of the law enforcers were described as having 'no parallel in the history of the city since the dreadful days of Peterloo'.

On 8 August, the three men appeared at the Minshull Street Court. They faced a charge of causing an obstruction of the traffic in Market Street and of obstructing the police in carrying out their duty. Then men were ordered to pay £50 and to keep the peace for twelve months. Later that year the government refreshed the Unemployed Workmen Bill and instated a Royal Commission on the poor laws.

The actions of the government provided a temporary fix to the plight of the unemployed, however it would not be enough to stop protests altogether in Manchester, which continued to make the headlines until 1911.

William Edward Skivington, one of the city's biggest supporters of the unemployed, died in 1910. He was only 42 years old and left behind his wife Ada and a daughter.

1913

MANCHESTER'S SUFFRAGETTES

SHORTLY AFTER 8.30 P.M. on 3 April 1913, suffragettes Annie Briggs, Lillian Forrester and Evelyn Manesta entered Manchester Art Gallery. As it was shortly before closing – it closed at 9 p.m. – the gallery was nearly empty. An attendant who was working inside heard the sound of breaking glass from room five. After dashing in – thinking a robbery was taking place – he was confronted by the three women wielding hammers and smashing the glass in all the pictures on display. The attendant quickly locked the door and called the police. Once the women realised they were locked in and the police had been called they put up no resistance.

Chief Constable Peacock and Superintendent Walker arrived on the scene with a group of officers. The women were then apprehended and

Manchester Art Gallery, 1900.

transferred to the Town Hall. All three were charged with 'unlawfully and maliciously damaging paintings in a gallery' and granted bail. In total the women had caused damage to thirteen pictures, which included work by George Frederic Watts, Dante Gabriel Rossetti, John Everett Millais, Briton Rivière, Studwick, Arthur Hacker, Holman Hunt and Frederic Leighton.

While the ladies were being interviewed by the police, uncorked bottles of an unknown black liquid had been placed in eleven postboxes in the districts of Ardwick, Longsight and Old Trafford by other suffragettes. Wrapped around the bottles were messages including 'Votes for Women', 'No Remedy till Votes for Women' and 'Down with the Tyrants'. In total it was estimated that 350 letters were damaged by the liquid. Those that could not be delivered were deposited at the Newton Street depot. The most affected areas were south-east Manchester, south-west Manchester and north and south Levenshulme. The culprits were never caught.

The attacks were believed to be in retaliation for the sentencing that day of suffragette leader Emmeline

Pankhurst. Mrs Pankhurst was born in Moss Side, Manchester, in 1858. Born into a wealthy politically active family, Emmeline was first introduced to the women's suffrage movement at the age of 12 when she went with her mother to hear Lydia Becker speak. However, it was not until her marriage to barrister Richard Pankhurst that she really got involved in politics, when she founded the Women's Franchise League. Five years after the death of her husband in 1898, Mrs Pankhurst and her daughters Christabel and Sylvia founded the Women's Social and Political Union (WSPU). The women operated out of their home on Nelson Street, Rusholme. It was not until 1906 that Christabel decided to take the party down the singular path of votes for women. After witnessing a successful demonstration by unemployed workers in Manchester which appeared to frighten the government into reform, Christabel believed that this tactic could work for women's suffrage. From that day forward the group took a more militant stance, with Christabel earning herself a seven-day prison sentence at Strangeways for disturbing a Liberal meeting attended by Winston Churchill and Sir Edward Grey.

By the time of the disturbance at the Manchester Art Gallery, the suffragettes had already conducted various head-line-grabbing demonstrations across the country. On the morning of the Manchester attacks, Mrs Pankhust was in the dock at the Old Bailey charged with 'feloniously procuring and inciting a person or persons unknown to commit a felony'. After hearing all the evidence, Pankhurst was given time to respond. In her long defence she argued that

Emmeline Pankhurst being arrested in 1914.

she would not plead guilty because she was being charged with 'wickedly and maliciously inciting' and she stated that she was neither wicked nor malicious. She further claimed that if she went to prison she would go on hunger strike.

After a short deliberation and to the outcry of suffragettes across the country, Mrs Pankhurst was found guilty and sentenced to three years' penal servitude. She was released on a special license after only four weeks.

While Mrs Pankhurst was serving time in Holloway Prison, the three art gallery vandals appeared at the Manchester Spring Assize. Forty-eight-year-old housekeeper Annie Briggs, 25-year-old governess Evelyn Manesta and 33-year-old Lillian Forrester faced a charge of 'malicious damaging'. After hearing all of the evidence Briggs was found not guilty, however Forrester and Manesta were found guilty. Both women seized the opportunity to give speeches in an attempt to defend their actions. It was reported that Forrester's speech lasted in the region of thirty minutes. During her defence she stated that the action of finding the courage to go into an art gallery and committing the act, and then being faced with the police and a trial, should be punishment enough. She then went on to suggest that there was a double standard of justice for 'powerful men and another for women who had no political status'. After passing the verdict the judge sentenced Forrester to three months in prison with two sureties of £25 and good behaviour for twelve months. Manesta was sentenced to one month in prison and two sureties of £25 and one year of good behaviour. The ladies were told that if they could not afford to pay the sureties their sentence would be increased.

GEORGE ALBERT STRINGER VC

ON **24 JULY 1889,** George Stringer and Esther Hewitt Pendleton welcomed their second son George Albert Stringer into the world. At the time of his birth George and Esther were living on Commerce Street. Esther was a native of New South Wales, however her parents were born in Lancashire. The family moved to Australia in 1855, before returning in 1870. Esther's father worked as a brickmaker and it is likely that this is how she met George, who was employed as a bricklayer's labourer.

Esther and George had twelve children during their marriage, however four of the children died in infancy, leaving four girls and four boys. The four sons were named James William, George Albert, Peter and William. All the boys attended the Albert Memorial School in Collyhurst.

In 1908, George Albert married Florence Marie Thornhill in

George Albert Stringer VC (1889–1957).

Manchester. By 1911, they were living at Lodge Street, in the Queens Road district of the city. George Albert was employed as a stover at Kerr, Hoeggers dyers and bleachers in Newton Heath. The rest of his family were living on Bath Street, Miles Platting. His brother James William was away at sea on board HMS *Victory*. In 1913, James William married Ada Knipe and the following year the couple would welcome a son named James after his father.

At the start of the First World War, all the Stringer boys enlisted. George Albert joined the 8th (Ardwick) Territorial Battalion of the Manchester Regiment; James William enlisted with the Royal Flying Corps; Peter joined the Loyal North Lancashire Regiment and William joined the 6th Kings Own Scottish Borders Regiment. As Esther waved her sons off into battle, she did so without knowing that it would be the last time that she would see two of them. Peter and James William would be dead by the end of November 1916. William and George Albert survived the war, however it would be George that would be most remembered out of all of the Stringer brothers.

On 8 March 1916, George Albert was stationed with his battalion in Mesopotamia. The Manchester Regiment were there to push back the

Ottoman forces in the city of Dujaila and relieve the British forces. The offensive became known as the Battle of Dujaila. During the battle the 1st Battalion of the Manchesters suffered heavy losses, however they managed to keep pushing forward and eventually reached the trenches of Dujaila with the 59th Rifles. Their success did not last long. A further Ottoman attack drove the troops from their trenches and back to their starting position. While the Manchesters were retreating, Private Stringer stayed on his own for over an hour, throwing grenades at the advancing Turkish soldiers and giving his troops a chance to withdraw, an act of bravery that saw him awarded the Victoria Cross. The details of George's award were described by Lieutenant Colonel Clive Wigram:

> For most conspicuous bravery and determination. After the capture of an enemy position he was posted on the extreme right of his battalion to guard against hostile attack. His battalion was subsequently forced back by an enemy counter-attack, but Private Stringer held his ground single-handed, and kept back the enemy till all his grenades were expended. His very gallant stand saved the flank of his battalion, and rendered a steady withdrawal possible.

The battles in Mesopotamia were deemed a failure for the British forces, which suffered severe losses and saw the town of Kut-al-Amara surrender to the Ottoman troops. In April 1916, the Manchesters left the Ottoman Empire and travelled to Egypt.

On 10 June 1917, Stringer arrived back in England, where he was greeted by his wife and family. Once word was out that he was back in Manchester, Stringer was treated as a local hero. His picture and story graced the pages of the local press. His former work colleagues at Kerr and Hoegger, dyers and bleachers on Grimshaw Lane held a soiree in his honour. He was presented with a marble clock, two bronze statues, war savings certificates and a sum of money by Mr Hoegger. The guests were then treated to some tea. On 9 July 1917, a public presentation was held to celebrate the VC hero at Brookdale Park. The events were hosted by Mr Cylnes MP. George Albert was given a writing desk and a smoking desk by the MP as a personal gift. Later that day he appeared at another presentation, this time held at his old school, Albert Memorial School in Oldham Road. He was presented with a gold watch and chain from the Old Boys' Union. He also received a barometer, a silver matchbox and a cigarette case from the teachers of the school, presented by Sir Thomas Shann.

On 21 July, Stringer was invited to Buckingham Palace to meet the king and receive his VC. He took with him his wife and parents. The king thanked him for his work in Mesopotamia and asked him if he had been wounded, due to the fact that he looked 'ill'. Stringer replied he had not, although he was suffering from 'fever and yellow jaundice'. He then told the king that when he was well again he hoped to go back to duty, to which the king replied, 'I thank you'.

George Albert Stringer never did return to active duty. He died on 22 November 1957 at Oldham General Hospital. He is buried with his mother and wife, who died two years after him, in a family plot at Philip's Park Cemetery.

1928

THE SHOOTING AT THE CLUB

ON 12 SEPTEMBER 1908, a postmaster's son named Alfred George Mace married Emily Juaneta Comish, the daughter of a sea captain. The lovebirds had met in Manchester where Emily was working as a nurse. Born in 1883, Alfred had lived in the city his whole life. From an early age it was evident that something was wrong with Alfred. As he grew, his spine did not form properly, leaving him with a hunched back. However, the disability did not stop him from succeeding in life. He and his family were very keen bowls players, with Alfred winning several trophies. He went on to become the director of the Manchester Athletics Grounds Committee, which owned the ground of the Manchester Athletics Club.

Alfred was also a keen businessman. At the age of 18 he progressed from an estate agent's clerk to a commission agent. He had two offices, in Clarence Street and West Didsbury. Alfred also owned a tobacconists and a hairdresser's shop in the city.

Shortly after their marriage, Alfred and Emily left Manchester and moved to Southport, where they kept a summer house. The nature of Alfred's business meant that he often went back to Manchester. It was on one of these trips

that he met a man named Joseph Fenton. Born in 1895, Fenton was employed as a bookmaker's clerk and lived in Fallowfield with his wife Emmaline and their young child. The nature of their relationship is unknown, however in the spring of 1928 Joseph Fenton left Manchester and arrived at the home of Alfred Mace in Southport. Fenton claimed that Alfred had had an affair with a waitress and had used his office as the place where the couple would meet. To keep his silence and to stop him telling Alfred's wife, the bookmaker's clerk demanded £200. Not wanting to be held to ransom, Alfred decided to tell his wife. After he had told Emily, he informed Fenton that he would not be paying him the money.

In the months prior to October 1928, Fenton began drinking heavily and appeared to his wife to be 'a bundle of nerves'. He also spoke about dying. Alfred, on the other hand, kept on about his business, making regular trips to Manchester. On Tuesday, 23 October, Alfred finished his work and arranged to meet his friend David William Lever. Lever worked as a draper and lived in Moss Side. The pair arranged to meet shortly after 5.30 p.m. at the Temperance Billiard Rooms, which was just off Albert Square and only a short distance from the city's Police Headquarters. Sometime after 7.30 p.m., Joseph Fenton arrived at the Billiard Rooms. In his hands were two pistols, a .45 Webley and a .22 automatic. Upon seeing Alfred, he marched up to him and the pair began arguing. Fenton then aimed his gun and fired straight at Alfred, hitting him in the side of his chest. Alfred died instantly. Fenton then turned

A depiction of Alfred George Mace playing billiards.

Picturesque Southport, c. 1900, where Alfred George Mace had his summer house and was buried.

his attention to Lever, who was trying in vain to stop him from shooting by throwing billiard balls, chairs, cues and any other missiles he could find at him. However, it was not enough to stop him. Lever was hit three times in the legs and body. Also caught in the crossfire was the son of the licensee of the premises, who narrowly avoided death after a bullet went through the neck of his coat, missing his throat by millimetres.

After the bullets were fired, Fenton made his escape. Outside waiting for him was his Singer four-seater car. As he drove off, the police arrived at the scene. Immediately the hunt began for the killer. Lever, meanwhile, was transferred to the infirmary.

Fenton was now on the run. Reports reached the officers that his car was heading in the direction of Sheffield, so the force targeted their resources in that area. Meanwhile, two unarmed officers from Manchester were sent to Fenton's home in Withington in case he was to return. Sometime after 10.30 p.m., Fenton returned home.

As he entered his front door he spotted the two officers and immediately drew his gun and pointed it at the men. With no weapons, the officers tried to talk to him, but he continued to threaten them. One of the officers then removed a silver cigarette box from his coat and pretended it was a gun. Spooked, Fenton made a dash to his bedroom and blocked the door. He then wrote an entry in his diary that was addressed to wife. It read, 'I didn't want to finish Mace and Lever. Just a lesson between the moral right and wrong and not to trifle with unknown quantities. Good-bye, Joe.' After writing the entry, Fenton took off his clothes and got into bed. He then picked up his gun, aimed it at his temple and fired a shot. He died instantly. David William Lever died five days later in the infirmary.

Alfred George Mace's funeral took place the following Monday in Southport. It was attended by his family, friends and members of the Manchester Commission Agents Association and the Imperial Bowling Club.

1933

MURDER IN THE FRONT ROOM

IN FEBRUARY 1933, 17-year-old Freda left her family in Durham and travelled to Manchester to find a job in service. Not long after she arrived in the city she managed to secure her first position working for a wealthy lady named Frances Levin, who lived in a large three-storey house on Cheetham Hill Road. Although Frances's husband spent the vast majority of his time in Ireland, Frances shared the house with her two daughters and two brothers.

Wednesday, 19 July 1933 started like every other day. Frances woke up, got dressed and ate her breakfast, prepared by her maid, Freda. At lunchtime she dined with one of her brothers and daughters, who saw her count the money in her purse, which totalled 9s. After lunch the girls left, however her brother did not leave till 2.30 p.m.

Sometime during that day, Frances had her bins emptied, meaning that the back door of the house was unlocked and the latch was left off the gate in the garden. Normally after lunch on a Wednesday, Frances would go for a drive in a motor car, however on this day she cancelled at the last minute and decided to go and rest in the front room. At roughly 3 p.m., Freda recalled taking some magazines and newspapers in for

Frances to read. Freda then went to her room – which was upstairs on the third floor – to do some sewing. The maid had been upstairs for about an hour when she saw a man enter the side passage near the house and stroll up the front drive. She described him as being about 5ft 8in tall, wearing a dark brown coat with dark trousers and a brown-coloured trilby. Due to her position upstairs and the tilt of his hat, she couldn't see his face; all she managed to catch was a glimpse of his chin.

Freda was not immediately alarmed by the strange man because she thought it was the man who had visited the house a few weeks previously to enquire about some chickens. So she carried on sewing. Over three quarters of an hour passed before Freda went downstairs. As she entered the kitchen she was confronted by a horrifying sight. On the floor was a poker covered in blood. Next to it was a stained shirt. Fearing something terrible had happened, Freda rushed outside and sought the help of next door's chauffeur, who was cleaning the cars. The chauffeur – a man named Norman Woodcock – ran into the house, accompanied by Freda. As they reached the front room they found the door closed. The chauffeur opened the door and walked into the room, while

Freda waited outside. Inside he found Frances lying on the sofa. Her head was covered in blood and she wasn't moving. Without a moment to waste, Norman conveyed the news to Freda and the pair ran to the telephone box to get help. Frances was then transferred to the Victoria Memorial Jewish Hospital, where she later died of a fractured skull.

When the police arrived at the scene, they conducted a thorough search of the house. They concluded the motive for the crime was probably robbery. Although nothing in the house was disturbed it appeared that there was money missing from Frances's purse. Due to the position of her body, they argued that she was probably asleep when she was attacked. The police removed the poker and the shirt for fingerprinting, however due to the nature of the materials, they were unable to extract any prints.

The search for the attacker spread far and wide. The police visited nearly every lodging house and pub in the city trying to find the killer. There were reports of a man matching the description in Wallasey, however when the police went to interview him it turned out to be a false alarm. Two porters from the Exchange Station reported seeing a man who arrived by taxi and appeared 'agitated'. The man had reached the station shortly after 9 p.m. and wanted to know what time the train to Warrington departed. The police appealed for the man and the taxi driver to come forward, but they were never found. A breakthrough finally came a week later when a tip-off from one of the residents led them to a man called William Burtoft. Burtoft was in his forties, had one eye

and was an out-of-work sailor. He had no fixed address, instead he stayed at various lodging houses throughout the city. Burtoft was eventually apprehended in Hyde and taken to Manchester Town Hall. While under the influence of methylated spirit, he gave a statement to the police in which he admitted being the killer. He stated that he was 'cool, calm and collected' when he walked into the front room. He further said that the 'old lady' stood up and enquired who he was, and with that he 'struck her repeatedly'. After the crime he said he went to Kane's lodging house in Angel Meadow and washed his hands. He then flushed his handkerchief down the toilet and walked to Swan Street to get some tea, before catching a tram to Oldham. After his confession, Burtoft was charged and sent for trial. He first appeared at the Manchester Police Court on 3 August 1933. The defending solicitor tried to get the statement thrown out of court as it was made while Burtoft was under the influence of methylated spirit, however the magistrate allowed the statement to be read. Burtoft pleaded not guilty and the case was then transferred to the assize.

The culprit was apprehended and taken to Manchester Town Hall.

The trial at the assize was not heard till November and lasted for two days. Burtoft refused to take the stand, with his solicitor arguing that it was his right not to talk and it was for the prosecution to prove his guilt. After hearing all the evidence, the jury took just over two hours to find him guilty and he was sentenced to death. His defence immediately launched an appeal, stating that there was no other evidence apart from the 'confession' of guilt. Even an identity parade in front of Freda failed to confirm him as the man that she had seen.

On 4 December the case was heard and dismissed at the Criminal Court of Appeal. Burtoft's execution took place at Strangeways Prison on 19 December 1933, exactly six months to the day of the murder. At his post-mortem the coroner remarked: 'Murder is not the sin of sins. Adultery is a sin against the soul. Hypocrisy is our natural sin, and apostasy, which is treason against Heaven, is the unforgivable sin.'

1940

THE CHRISTMAS BLITZ

A T 11.15 A.M. on 3 September 1939, families across Manchester were gathered around the wireless to hear an address from Prime Minister Neville Chamberlain. Chamberlain confirmed what the nation had feared. The deadline for Germany to withdraw its troops from Poland had passed and Britain was now at war with Germany. Although the news was not what the vast majority of the public wanted to hear, Manchester had been preparing for war for the previous two years. In 1937 an appeal had been made for people to assist with air-raid precautions and by March 1938 it was reported that the city had received over 8,000 applications, with over 2,000 people volunteering as air-raid wardens and

Parker Street, taken after the Blitz.
(Reproduced with the kind permission of
Manchester City Council, MO4324)

over 1,200 volunteering as auxiliary firemen. On 26 February 1938, the city officially got its first air-raid shelter on Mount Street. The shelter could hold fifty people and would protect them from a gas attack for between six and twelve hours. Estimates suggested that Manchester would need at least 500 shelters to protect the citizens from a potential bomb attack.

Officials in Manchester knew that due to its geographical location and its industrial links to the war effort, the city – like most industrial cities – would be a key target in Hitler's bombing campaign. This led them to ensure that by the time the war broke out in 1939, evacuations had already started. The city's children were the first to leave. Corporation buses and special trains transported over 70,000 children to rural destinations such as Cheshire, Yorkshire and Derbyshire.

By the time 1940 arrived, Manchester had seen little in the way of German bombers. This changed in the summer of 1940. The first air-raid warning was sounded in the city at 3.14 a.m. on 20 June 1940. Although the sound of German aircraft could be heard, there were no reports of bombing.

Throughout the summer and autumn, the city was subjected to a series of small bombing raids, which caused little more than structural damage. By 8 December, Manchester University, the College of Technology, the Palace Theatre, the New Hippodrome, the Apollo Cinema, Ardwick Wrestling Stadium and Salford Town Hall had all been hit by bombs. Some of the damage was only minor and the local media reported how 'remarkably ineffective' the German campaign had been. However, things in Manchester were about to change.

On 20 December 1940, and for the following three nights, German bombs fell upon Liverpool. The devices hit the docks, municipal buildings – including the Town Hall – the Cunard offices, as well as several residential areas. To help in the clean-up effort, Manchester sent over 200 firemen. On 22 December, while the firemen where assisting in Liverpool, the Germans were planning their next attack. This time their target

The remains of Miller Street after the bombs had hit, December 1940. (Reproduced with the kind permission of Manchester City Council, MO3357)

was Manchester. Shortly after 6.30 p.m. the sirens rang out over the city. People had barely enough time to get in the shelters before incendiaries and high explosives started falling on the city. Wave after wave of bombing continued for the next twelve hours. The first group of bombs were dropped in the district of Albert Square. A building on the corner of Princess Street was one of the first to be hit. Bombs were then dropped on Bridgewater Street. The Royal Exchange was hit and set ablaze. A tailor's shop on the corner of Corporation Street was also on fire. Warehouses on Portland Street and Watson Street were ablaze. Victoria Buildings was hit and a part of it collapsed, blocking Deansgate. Bombs also hit residential districts, damaging over 30,000 houses. In one area of the city 341 people were forced to take refuge in the Wood Street Mission. Mixed in with the bombs were leaflets with a message from Hitler entitled 'Hitler's last appeal to reason'.

As Manchester began assessing the damage, the German bombers were loading their aeroplanes for a second attack. At 7.15 p.m. on 23 December, the booms started again. The last bomb was dropped at 6 a.m. It hit the north-east corner of the cathedral. The impact shook the whole building and lifted the roof. All the windows and doors were blown out. The altar was reduced to a pile of rubble and the two organs were broken into bits. It was estimated that over 280 high explosives and over 1,000 incendiaries were dropped over the city during the two nights. It took till the early hours of Christmas Eve before all the fires in the city were under control. In total 165 warehouses were damaged, five banks were destroyed, 100 schools were damaged and 500 businesses were affected. Buildings such as the Free Trade Hall, Victoria Buildings, and Cross Street chapel were reduced to rubble.

The loss to human life was substantial with hundreds dying and over 723 people being treated for injuries.

Six days after the bombing had started, the unclaimed dead were buried in a public grave in Southern Cemetery.

Hundreds of mourners attended the service, which included representatives from all religious denominations. In total seventy-two people were buried that day in the public service. The Bishop of Manchester addressed the mourners and declared: 'Death may come; death came to you. Death has come to Manchester. But there shall come in His faith a sure resurrection; there is no ground for despair; there is assurance of victory.'

1947

ANTI-JEWISH RIOTS

ON 12 JULY 1947, two British soldiers named Sergeant Mervyn Paice and Sergeant Clifford Martin were kidnapped with force whilst out with a friend in the British-occupied region of Palestine. The men were beaten and later executed by a group of terrorist fighters called the Irgun. It was claimed by the organisation that their murders were in retaliation for three of their fighters, who had been convicted of an attack on the Acre Jail and sentenced to death.

After word reached the British Army that their comrades had been killed, a hunt got underway to discover the men's bodies and find the perpetrators. This was made particularly difficult due to a wall of silence from the locals who were protecting the murderers. It would take the British forces three weeks to eventually find the deceased soldiers. When the army finally reached the men, their attempts to retrieve the bodies were severely hampered by a series of mines that had been placed on one of the victims.

The day after the discovery, on 1 August – which was the Friday Bank Holiday – the *Daily Express* released a picture of the two soldiers hanging from a tree. The story outraged and shocked the nation. Up and down the country people were discussing the murder of the two soldiers. In Manchester, Liverpool, London, as in other parts of the country, discussions soon became heated, resulting in widespread rioting. The anger of the people seemed to be directed at the Jewish residents and businesses in the cities.

The worst of the riots began in Manchester and Salford on Saturday. Angry mobs, containing a mixture of soldiers and civilians, made their way around the city damaging property owned by Jewish residents. On Rochdale Road, bricks were thrown from car windows and a window of a Jewish business was shattered. Police dealt with disturbances that night in Strangeways, Brunswick Street, Rusholme and Cheetham Hill Road. After hearing that a Jewish meeting was taking place at the Assembly Rooms, a mob of over 100 people descended on the venue. The panicked people inside – who had been enjoying dancing and socialising – were forced to wait until the mob had left before they could make their escape. In Derby Street, a furious crowd gathered on the corner of Cheetham Hill Road. The majority were teenagers, who seemed intent on causing damage to shop windows. Windows were also smashed in Jewish shops on Petworth Street and Heywood Street. Crowds gathered in Broad Street, Cross Lane and Regent Road.

Shouts of 'We ought to do what Hitler did', and 'Down with the Jews' were reported in the local press. The crowds smashed windows of Jewish businesses, including the shop of Montague Burton on Broad Street, although at times the mob appeared to just guess the religion of the shop owner. Two teenage girls were caught abusing the guests at a Jewish wedding. When the police arrived the girls refused to move so were taken into custody. A Jewish man who watched the disturbances was knocked to the floor and needed treatment at the Manchester Victoria Jewish Hospital, eventually making a full recovery.

Reports of fighting were also reported throughout the city. Non-Jewish and Jewish ex-servicemen got into a scuffle outside the British Legion on Queens Road. Tensions were heightened to such a degree that in the city an argument broke out in the queue of the New Oxford Cinema when someone decided to bring up the subject of Palestine. The argument would have quickly developed into a fight had it not been for the swift actions of the cinema manager who called 999. The police arrived just before the first punch was thrown, and they quickly managed to disperse the angered men. The police drafted in special constables and operated a policy of 'moving on' and dispersing any crowds that were found to be loitering on the streets. With this they had relative success in preventing anyone from getting seriously injured. However, they had failed to stop the unprecedented damage to Jewish shops and businesses. Manchester's police force were not the only city force trying to keep the peace: Liverpool's Jewish community was also

under attack. Rioters set fire to a synagogue and factory, shops were looted and windows were smashed at many Jewish-owned businesses. In Birkenhead, slaughterhouse workers stopped producing meat for Jewish retailers until 'their country stopped attacking British soldiers'. In Eccles town centre, near Manchester, over £1,000 worth of damage was caused by the rioters. In total five men were charged. The longest sentence was given to a 38-year-old man named Jack Piggot, who was found guilty of causing £40 in damages and was sentenced to six months in prison.

In Manchester, 21-year-old Thomas Walker was found guilty of breaking a shop window and was sentenced to four months in prison. John Shrine was sentenced to two months in prison after the magistrate failed to believe that he just 'fell on the window and it smashed'.

After a weekend of rioting and a series of political messages condemning the attacks, the city recovered and the Jewish community continued to thrive in Manchester. Britain left Palestine in 1948, which signalled the termination of the British Mandate. The murdered military officers – Sergeant Clifford Martin and Sergeant Mervyn Paice – were buried at Ramla British Military Cemetery in Israel.

Shop windows were smashed in Jewish communities across the city during the riots.

IMAGE CREDITS

Images listed by page number:

BIBLIOGRAPHY

Books

Briggs, A., *Victorian Cities* (London: Penguin, 1990)

Cavendish, R., Leahy, P., *Kings and Queens* (Cincinnati: David &Charles, 2008)

Engels, F., *The Condition of the Working-Class in England in 1844* (London: George Allen & Unwin, 1943)

Hartwell, C., *Manchester* (London: Yale University Press, 2002)

Hulme, M., *A Grim Almanac of Manchester* (Stroud, The History Press, 2015)

Hylton, S., *A History of Manchester* (Chichester: Phillimore, 2003)

Jones, G.D.B., *Roman Manchester* (Altrincham: John Sherratt & Son, 1974)

Kidd, A., *Manchester: A History* (Lancaster: Carnegie Publishing, 2008)

Marlow, J., *The Peterloo Massacre* (London: Granada Publishing Ltd, 1971)

Messinger, G.S., *Manchester in the Victorian Age* (Manchester: Manchester University Press, 1985)

Morris, M., *Medieval Manchester Volume 1* (Manchester: Greater Manchester Archaeological Unit, 1983)

Reilly, J., *History of Manchester* (London: Judd & Glass, 1865)

Storey, N.R., *The Victorian Criminal* (Oxford: Shire Library, 2011)

Thomson, W.H., *History of Manchester to 1852* (John Sharratt & Son, 1967)

Websites

www.ancestry.co.uk
www.burialrecords.manchester.gov.uk
www.executedtoday.com
www.findmypast.co.uk
www.lancastercastle.com
www.proquest.com

Other Sources

Court Leet Records 1552–1686 (Manchester: Henry Blacklock & Co., 1888)

Court Leet Records 1731–1846 (Manchester: Henry Blacklock & Co., 1888)

England & Wales, Criminal Registers, 1791–1892 (www.ancestry.co.uk)

Manchester Courier and Lancashire General Advertiser (1825–1916)

Manchester Guardian (1821–1950)

Manchester Historical Recorder (1874)

Manchester Mercury (1759–1826)

Manchester Times (1828–1900)

Our Blitz (Kemsley Newspapers)

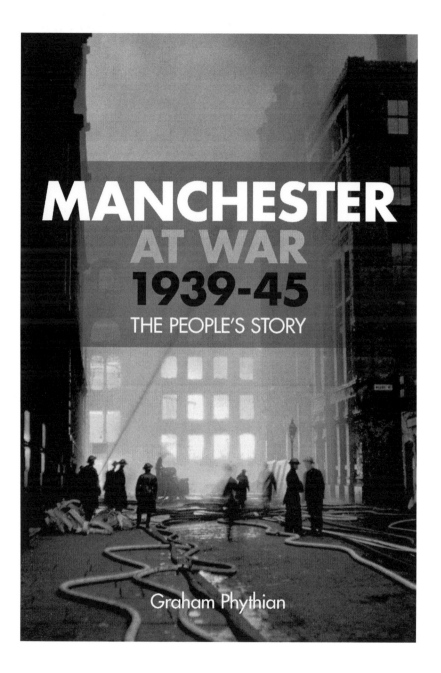